SUCCESS IN MARRIAGE

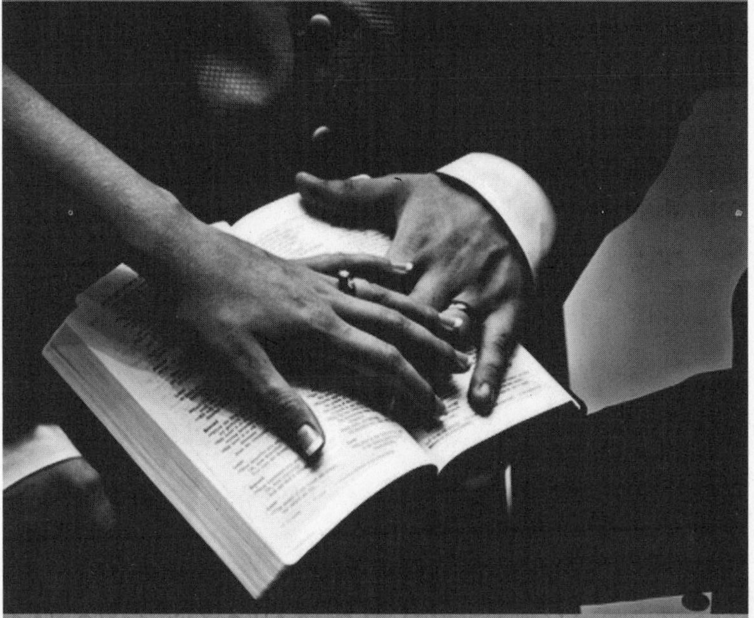

DAVID & FAITH OYEDEPO

Success in Marriage

Re-edited June 2013

ISBN 978-2480-84-3

Published in Nigeria by:

DOMINION PUBLISHING HOUSE

For further information or permission, please contact:

DOMINION PUBLISHING HOUSE

Canaan Land, Km 10, Idiroko Road, Ota.

P.M.B. 21688, Ikeja, Lagos State, Nigeria.

Tel: 234-1-7747546-8

Web: www.davidoyedepoministries.org,

www.faithoyedepo.org;

E-mail: dph@davidoyedepoministries.org

All scripture quotations are from the King James Version of the Bible, except otherwise stated.

CONTENTS

The Commission

"The hour has come to liberate the world from all oppressions of the devil, through the preaching of the Word of Faith, and I am sending you to undertake this task."

Preface

When I was growing up, I did not see many successful marriages around. As a result, I had many questions which I needed to find answers to, before entering into marriage. I believe strongly in purpose, so I needed to know God's purpose for instituting marriage and to be sure that it is not a necessary evil as many have today accepted it to be, but honourable and glorious.

So, I settled down to a search — studying and meditating on the Word of God. It was in the course of one of those deep meditations that I located seven fundamental truths about marriage, which I called the seven concepts of marriage. I discovered that as the "manufacturer" of marriage, God had reasons for creating this "product."

Success in marriage, as in any other endeavour in life, answers to working, not dreaming. A wise man once said that some people dream of success, while others wake up and work hard at it. Also, an adage says, "If wishes were horses, beggars would ride." So, success in marriage is not wished for, but worked at.

Every achievement in life is worked for. Nothing works itself, just like no problem solves itself. For instance, a student who wants to fail spends all night praying, instead of doing his assignments and studying. Prayer does not take the place of actually bending down to do the assignment; it only complements it.

Even miracles answer to certain inputs from the benefactor. Your obedience to what is required of you is how you initiate it. Take the miracle of the turning of water into wine, for instance. Mary told the men, "*Whatever he tells you to do, do it*." The servants initiated their miracle by obeying Jesus' instructions to fill the water-pots with water.

A testimony I once heard further proved to me that marriage miracles do not drop down like apples from a tree, as some believe, but are the result of certain deliberate acts of men. A brother wanted to gun down his wife just a year earlier. But he caught some insights from the Word of God, applied them, and they are both having a second honeymoon now!

Nothing happens by chance in the Kingdom of God.

There is something you must do, to enjoy a hitch-free marriage. All you need do is to accept the required responsibility.

As an adult, I expect you to ask, "Lord, what must I do to be successful in marriage?" It is children who are always on the begging side, saying, "Give me, give me. God do this, God do that." A mature person should seek the way out of whatever predicament he finds himself. The Bible says in 1 Corinthians 10:13:

> ***There hath no temptation taken you but such as is common to man: but God is faithful, who will not suffer you to be tempted above that ye are able; but will with the temptation also make a way to escape, that ye may be able to bear it.***

Notice that God's responsibility is to provide a way of escape for you; but He leaves it to you to locate and follow that way. Your wife cannot be the worst person in the world, neither is your husband the devil you claim he is. Yours is simply a case of ignorance! The devil's success in troubling your home is only due to your ignorance. God told me sometime ago that there is no mountain anywhere, that every man's ignorance is his mountain.

So, I see you levelling the mountains before you, through the knowledge you will contact in this book.

Open up to God, and ask Him to show you the way out of those marital problems. Once He does, and you do what He says, you have committed Him to ensure that your home is established in peace and harmony.

– David Oyedepo

Introduction

I am excited about writing this book on marriage in collaboration with my husband. I believe that the revelations God gave him on marriage years before we were married, and which have worked for us, need to be shared.

Our marriage has been very exciting. I have tasted God's goodness in it, and I must say that I am thoroughly enjoying myself. I often humorously say that although the Bible makes it very clear that there is no marriage in heaven (and I believe it), but I believe my mansion will be next to my husband's, when we finally get to heaven! I can't imagine what heaven will be like for me otherwise.

Marriage is the legal union of a man and woman as husband and wife. It is the foundation for the family, because until it is in place, there can be no family. A family is a social group in society, consisting of a man, his wife and their offspring.

Marriage, as God intended, is meant to be exciting, fulfilling and exhilarating. If yours, by any chance, has lost its excitement or is falling short of God's intent, do not despair because God can impart His joy and goodness into it once again. He can still make something special out of your home. Part of the restoration process, is this book in your hands.

I saw something in Genesis 2:7, that changed my life.

> ***And the Lord God formed man of the dust of the ground, and breathed into his nostrils the breath of life; and man became a living soul.***

God made man out of dust, a valueless thing. No one goes out in search of dust. As a matter of fact, when your shoes gather a bit of dust, you wipe it off. That tells you just how valuable dust is. But as worthless as it is, God made something worthwhile out of it.

We can draw a spiritual parallel from this: no matter how worthless you regard your spouse, something glorious can still come out of him or her. You may think your marriage is valueless, but God can make something outstanding of it.

Not only that, God did not fold His arms after forming man from dust. He also breathed into his nostrils the breath of life, and man became a living soul. What transforms ordinary dust to a living soul is the breath of life. Isaiah 34:16 tells us what that breath is:

> ***Seek ye out of the book of the Lord, and read: no one of these shall fail, none shall want her mate: for my mouth it hath commanded, and his spirit it hath gathered them.***

I believe that the breath of life is what has been gathered together and compiled into the Bible. So, whatever is **revealed** in the Word and is **received** has the power to transform an ordinary man into an extraordinary person. The same is true concerning marriage. No matter how hopeless your home may seem now, when you open up to the Word of God, God will make a success out of it.

So many marriages are "dead" today, even though both parties are still living together. This could be due to the absence of the *"breath of life"* (the Word of God) in such marriages. As soon as that breath comes into your home, it will come alive. Just as Adam became a living soul by the breath of life, your marriage too will become a living marriage!

My greatest heart's desire for you, as you read this book and apply the principles therein, is that your home will come alive and become full of joy, laughter and excitement, as mine is. Come along with me as we explore how.

– Faith Oyedepo

One

The Covenant Of Marriage

- Faith

Marriage is a covenant relationship. It is not just the coming together of a man and woman for the purpose of procreation. Although having children is one of the blessings of marriage, marriage means much more than that. Some other people think marriage is merely cohabiting with someone of the opposite sex. Again, this perception is wrong, as marriage goes beyond that. Marriage is a Covenant.

God is a God of covenants. All through Scriptures, we see God in covenant relationships with different people.

Abraham

God cut a covenant with Abraham in Genesis chapter 17.

> ***And I will make my covenant between me and thee, and will multiply thee exceedingly.***
>
> Genesis 17:2

Although Abraham died thousands of years ago, the covenant God cut with him then is still in force today. Interestingly, we all are proud to be called children of Abraham today, even though we never met him in person. The covenant God cut with Abraham was sealed in blood, and the sign is circumcision.

Noah

> ***And I, behold, I establish my covenant with you, and with your seed after you;***
>
> ***I do set my bow in the cloud, and it shall be for a token of a covenant between me and the earth.***
>
> Genesis 9:9,13

God again cut a covenant with Noah in Genesis chapter 8. Noah took of all the clean beasts and sacrificed them, to seal up the covenant, after which God put the rainbow in the sky, as a sign of the immutability of the covenant.

Jesus Christ

> ***Likewise also the cup after supper, saying, This cup is the new testament in my blood, which is shed for you.***
>
> Luke 22:20

God kept cutting covenants with His people until Jesus, the only Begotten of the Father, came and enacted a new covenant (testament) in His blood.

What Is A Covenant?

A covenant is a bond. It is also a formal sealed agreement or contract with witnesses. God is the principal witness, while the people present are the cloud of witnesses.

A covenant is quite different from a promise. A promise is a declaration assuring that one will or will not do something; a vow. There are no conditions attached to it, unlike in a covenant.

The covenant of marriage is three-sided. It is first **horizontal,** then **parallel** and **vertical**. It is horizontal because it is a threefold responsibility between God as the source, and the man and his wife. Each of the couple must answer to God as an individual, in the fulfillment of God's command concerning them. Interestingly, the closer each party gets to God, the closer their relationship with each other also grows as the distance between them becomes narrower.

A. HORIZONTAL

Horizontally the covenant of marriage is between God and the couple. Take a close look at this graphic illustration.

GOD

(Malachi 3:6; II Timothy 2:13; Titus1:2, Hebrews 13:8)

Colossians 3:17

... do as unto The Lord. everyone playing their part independently

WIFE

Ephesians 5:22 (Submit as unto the Lord)

HUSBAND

Ephesians 5:25; 1 Timothy 5:8 (Love as unto the Lord)

Maritally, husband and wife are both answerable to God by covenant.

(a). **Man** - Malachi 2:14 - God is witness between Husband and Wife in marriage.

(b). **Woman** - Genesis 2:18 – God created you for a purpose and you will answer to Him for the fulfillment of that purpose.

B. PARALLEL

Parallel - wise, the covenant of marriage is between wife and husband.

Study this graphic illustration.

1 Corinthians 7:2-3, Ephesians 5:21

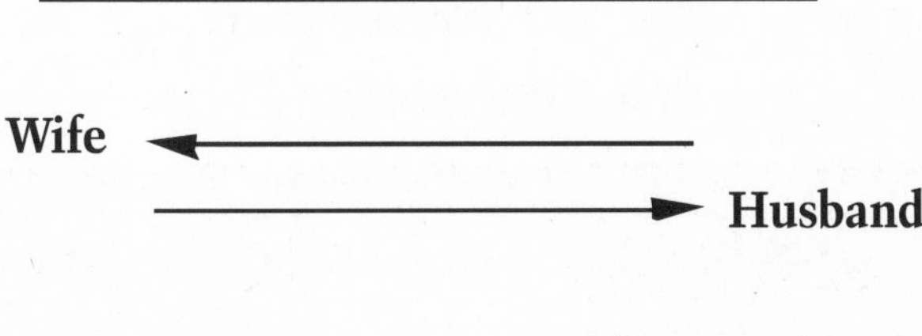

Husband and wife have covenant obligations to each other for which they will be held accountable.

C. VERTICAL

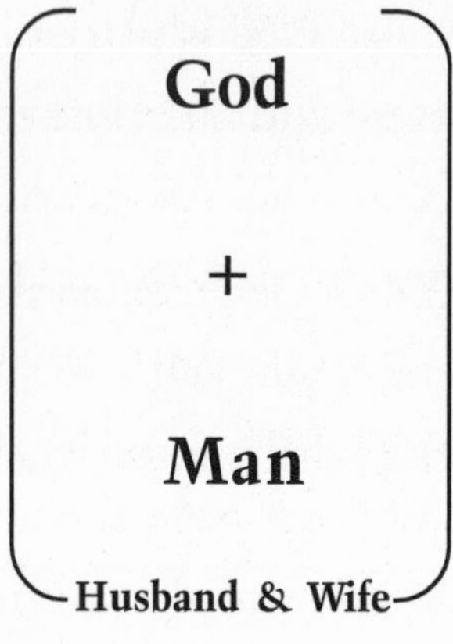

Before your vertical relationship can blossom, your horizontal and parallel relationship must first be in place.

As one flesh, the couple is also jointly accountable to God for their joint responsibilities.

The marriage covenant is also vertical in nature because it is between God and man (husband and wife). God's own side of the covenant is constant and settled. God is not more faithful in one marriage than another. He is no respecter of persons. What He does for one, He will do for another (Acts 10:34).

Many people get into marriage without understanding that it is a covenant. Instead, they keep wishing that it will become glorious. But because they have not fulfilled their own side of the deal, they never taste the glory in it.

A good **horizontal** relationship gives birth to an effective **parallel** relationship, and a good **parallel** relationship gives birth to an effective **vertical** relationship.

Your spouse is not just a bedmate or a friend, but is the *"wife of thy covenant"* (Malachi 2:14). In essence, you are in a covenant relationship with him or her. But this applies only to husband and wife. As a matter of fact, singles who are in courtships, must know that their courtship partners are not covenant partners; you don't owe him or her any covenant obligations until you're actually married. Do not let anyone put pressure on you. As long as you are not yet joined together in marriage, you are not bound by covenant, so, you are not in a covenant relationship.

I met a brother who had met a girl he wanted to marry. But the lady wanted them to enter into a blood covenant by cutting each other's flesh and drinking their blood to seal it up, claiming that they were in a marriage covenant. This is demonic! It shows a misconception of the subject of the covenant of marriage. That is not how to enter the marriage covenant.

The marriage covenant only comes into force, when you are legally joined together with your wife or husband in marriage. Because it is a covenant, you are expected to keep and not break it. You are made in God's image, and He is faithful to His covenants, He never breaks them. He said in Psalm 89:34:

My covenant will I not break, nor alter the thing that is gone out of my lips.

The Bible says:

...Therefore take heed to your spirit, and let none deal treacherously against the wife of his youth.

Malachi 2:15

The word "treacherous" connotes deception. God is saying, therefore, "Don't deal deceptively with your wife or husband." In some marriages, the man plans mischief against the woman, and she in turn looks for ways of robbing and cheating him. But that is ridiculous, because whatever you do against your spouse, you are indirectly doing against yourself!

Some people betray their partners to their extended families or friends. A traitor is the same as a treacherous man. I have seen people who betrayed their spouses and were also betrayed. Remember that the law of seedtime and harvest is still in force. What you sow is what you reap (Genesis 8:22).

Characteristics Of The Marriage Covenant

It is written

A marriage covenant is a formal declaration, usually

written and having witnesses. This is typically demonstrated in Joshua 24:25-27:

> ***So Joshua made a covenant with the people that day, and set them a statute and an ordinance in Shechem.***
>
> ***And Joshua wrote these words in the book of the law of God, and took a great stone, and set it up there under an oak, that was by the sanctuary of the LORD.***
>
> ***And Joshua said unto all the people, Behold, this stone shall be a witness unto us; for it hath heard all the words of the LORD which he spake unto us: it shall be therefore a witness unto you, lest ye deny your God.***
>
> Emphasis mine

Every valid covenant has not only to be written, but must be a writing that is enforceable. In Psalm 74:20-22, the Psalmist called on God to enforce the covenant He made with the people.

> ***Have respect unto the covenant: for the dark places of the earth are full of the habitations of cruelty.***
>
> ***O let not the oppressed return ashamed: ...***
>
> ***Arise, O God, plead thine own cause: ...***
>
> Psalm 74:20-22

The same is true for the marriage covenant. There is the need for you to put your commitment down in writing, by obtaining a marriage certificate issued from an authorized Church licensed to conduct weddings, or a Local Government declaration of marriage, which is legally binding and enforceable in our judicial system. To the woman, let me say this: if you are married and do not have a marriage certificate to prove that you are legally married, make sure you get one, as this will enable you to enter into a proper covenant.

Not only should the covenant be in writing, it must also be before witnesses. Severally in scriptures, we find instances of this. In Genesis 31:44-53:

> ***Now therefore come thou, let us make a covenant, I and thou; and let it be for a witness between me and thee.***
>
> ***... And Jacob said unto his brethren, Gather stones; and they took stones, and made an heap: ...***
>
> ***... And Laban said, This heap is a witness between me and thee this day. ... for he said, The LORD watch between me and thee, when we are absent one from another.***
>
> ***... God is witness betwixt me and thee.***
>
> ***And Laban said to Jacob, Behold this heap, and behold this pillar, ... This heap be witness, and this pillar be witness, that I will not pass over this heap to thee, and that thou shalt not pass over this heap and this pillar unto me, for harm.***

> ***The God of Abraham, and the God of Nahor, the God of their father, judge betwixt us.***

In **Malachi 2:14**, we see that God is the principal witness in the marriage covenant:

> ***The LORD hath been witness between thee and the wife of thy youth, against whom thou hast dealt treacherously: yet is she thy companion, and the wife of thy covenant.***

If God is a witness to your marriage covenant, then ensure you have respect to your part of the covenant by observing to do them.

It Should Not Be Broken

The marriage covenant should not be broken. God is a covenant keeper, not a covenant breaker (Psalm 89:34). As His children, therefore, husband and wife should be covenant keepers, not covenant breakers.

An important characteristic of the marriage covenant is that it is meant to be for life.

> ***The wife is bound by the law as long as her husband liveth; but if her husband be dead, she is at liberty to be married to whom she will; only in the Lord.***
>
> 1 Corinthians 7:39

The covenant of marriage is in force, as long as both parties (the man and the woman) are still alive. There is no room for divorce. Divorce is not a good experience. Only those who have experienced it can tell the experience. I consider it as marital amputation. You must do all within your power to avoid it. Even though God is a God of second chance, it is better to avoid divorce than to experience it. Divorce is like a shoot-out between Siamese twins. No matter what happens, both partners become casualties.

Once you are married, the question of separation should not arise. You must settle it within yourself that there are no alternatives, nowhere else to go. By entering into the covenant of marriage, you have burnt the bridge behind you. This simple understanding will help you settle down and make your home an exciting place.

So, the covenant of marriage is for life. May be you are married but are contemplating running away from your home because of the challenges before you now. Hold on a while. Remember that Malachi 2:16 says that God hates divorce, particularly if you are a believer, and your husband or wife is yet to become one. Don't run away, and don't give in to pressure.

You are the light of the world (Matthew 5:14), and light does not run away from darkness. Rather, it shines in darkness and darkness cannot comprehend it (John 1:5). So, stay put, and ensure that your light is not put under the bushel, but on the lamp stand, so it can shine in your home and shatter every form of darkness.

The covenant of marriage is meant to be in force till death. In case your spouse has already packed out and you desire a re-union with him or her, you can go to God and plead your case, instead of rushing out to re-marry. I have witnessed cases of amazing re-unions. Let me share a few of them with you.

"In 1970, my mother's marriage with my father broke down, because of another woman. When she visited me, she agreed to follow us to church. After seeing the power of God in the church, she waited for the October Breakthrough Seminar. God re-moulded her life in that period, because she had been a great problem to us.

When she was returning home, she took the 'Judgment Oil' with her; and I instructed her to always anoint her house and our house in the village. She did that. In December, both my father and mother attended my younger sister's wedding, and my father hugged her for the first time in 24 years! They are back together now, and he said he is now re-wedding his wife!" – **Ibe, C.**

"I was in the state of a broken marriage when I came to Abeokuta in 1986. At that time, I was living in frustration and fear, because my wife had packed out of our home. We had been married for 17 years when our

marriage broke up. She had even sued for a divorce and was granted one. Then she left me for another man that same year.

It was in this condition that I met Christ in 1991. All efforts to reconcile with my wife failed in the church where I gave my life to Christ, so I stopped going there. For two years I did not go to any church, before the Holy Spirit led me to this church (Winners') on January 7, 1996.

When I came to this church, I went to see one of the pastors who asked me about my wife. I told him we were separated. He prayed for me and asked me to write her. A month after I wrote the letter, I phoned her, because she works in a ministry in Lagos. Her response was good, because she never wanted to speak to me before I sent her the letter. I told her I would be coming to Lagos to see her and she agreed.

So, I went to Lagos. But before I went, I anointed myself and took a shot of the anointing oil. On getting to her office, she received me well and I met my second son there. My wife told me in the presence of my second son that she called all my children and showed them the letter I wrote her. She then said, 'There is no more misunderstanding between us.' Everyone in her office was just looking at us.

What surprised me most was that my wife was the one introducing me to people. Her boss, who also wanted us to be re-united, was very happy to see the two of us together. She prayed for us, that God would perfect what He had started in our lives. Since then, we have been in touch with one another. I thank God that my broken marriage has been restored!" **– Soetan, I. O.**

If truly you love your husband or wife, no matter the things done to hurt you before your separation, you will forgive him or her and pray, believing God for a re-union.

However, in case you are already divorced and all hope for a re-union is lost (probably your partner has remarried), the believing wife or husband is not held in bondage. Paul says it's better to marry than to burn:

> ***But if they cannot contain, let them marry: for it is better to marry than to burn.***
>
> ***But if the unbelieving depart, let him depart. A brother or a sister is not under bondage in such cases: but God hath called us to peace.***
>
> 1 Corinthians 7: 9,15

Exchange Of Gifts

Another feature which should be in place in any marriage is the exchange of gifts. We see an example of this in the covenant between God and Abraham. God asked Abraham for Isaac, and Abraham did not hesitate, neither did he bother about what Sarah was going to say, nor about Isaac's opinion. He knew he was in a covenant relationship with God and didn't want to break it. Because the covenant involves the exchange of gifts, he was willing to offer Isaac as a sacrifice to God (Genesis 22).

When a man is truly in a covenant relationship with a woman, there is nothing he cannot give to her, and vice versa. As a matter of fact, he or she should not need to ask for a thing; the partner should always look for ways of blessing his or her spouse.

There is nothing my husband and I cannot give to each other, because we both understand how the covenant of marriage works.

When two people are in the covenant of marriage, they ought to be committed to the good of one another. It is, however, amazing to see couples hiding money away from each other. Some conceal how much they earn, the property they have, etc, from their partner. But such acts reveal that they do not understand this vital characteristic of the marriage covenant.

Once married, all that a couple had before marriage now jointly belong to them. Don't allow material things to come between you and your spouse. When God created

Eve, He brought her to Adam, and the Garden of Eden was given to both of them. So husband and wife, don't withhold anything from one another. Never play hide-and-seek with your spouse, if you don't want shame (Genesis 2:25).

Sharing in marriage is so important that God gave only one name to Adam and his wife (Genesis 5:2). Have you ever wondered why husband and wife bear one name after marriage? Mr. and Mrs.—Sharing is the reason.

It Has A Seal

A covenant is usually sealed with blood and has a token or sign. Noah made a covenant with God in Genesis 8:20, and offered burnt offerings unto Him. God on His part also set a bow as a token of the covenant (Genesis 9:13).

In Genesis 17, the seal of Abraham's covenant with God is the circumcision of every male child.

> ***And ye shall circumcise the flesh of your foreskin; and it shall be a token of the covenant betwixt me and you.***
>
> Genesis 17:11

Jesus also shed His blood on the Cross of Calvary, as a seal of the covenant of salvation.

> ***But now hath he obtained a more excellent ministry, by how much also he is the mediator of a better***

covenant, which was established upon better promises.

Hebrews 8:6

Just as every covenant has a seal (a seal is among other things, "a confirming token, that which closes"), the seal of the marriage covenant is sexual intercourse.

The first meeting between husband and wife in marriage involves the shedding of blood, no matter how little. After this first meeting, subsequent sexual relationship between husband and wife is re-enacting the "token" of the marriage covenant.

A man's semen has a microscopic trace of blood in it. Therefore, each time he releases semen into his wife, his blood is shed, as it were, and life is represented in that union. So, in order not to be a covenant breaker, never get involved in a sexual relationship with anyone apart from your spouse. Sexual immorality is dangerous!

It Transcends Generations

Once a man and a woman get married, history is made, and they can never change that lineage. Generations after them will keep connecting them with that lineage, whenever reference is being made about them (Matthew 1:6). Be determined, therefore, to have a good history to leave behind for your generations to come. Be remembered for good.

Men and women in a marriage covenant are expected to observe and apply the above characteristics, so that their homes will last and be the havens they were created to be.

Two

God's Interest In The Family

– Faith

> ***For every house is builded by some man; but he that built all things is God.***
>
> Hebrews 3:4

The family unit is currently facing one of its greatest attacks today, more than at any other period in history. More than ever before, the family needs the help of God from the troubles, woes and calamities that befall it daily.

We have sought help from man — psychiatrists, traditional and political leaders, etc., only to find out that the help man claims to render is grossly inadequate.

Man is still looking here and there in search of lasting solutions to the problems encountered in marriage. But the Psalmist shows us the secret for an enduring solution:

> ***Give us help from trouble: for vain is the help of man.***
>
> Psalm 60:11

God's help is always available to us. God's help can reach you, no matter in what area of family life you desire it. I believe it is coming your way right now via this book. The degree of problems you have experienced in your marriage notwithstanding, God's help is actually all you need.

Although it is your responsibility to build your home, the ultimate builder is God (Hebrews 3:4). Whatever is built outside Him, therefore, has no future. In 2 Chronicles 26, we are told the story of king Uzziah, who became king at the age of 16, and reigned for 52 years. Verse 7 lets us into his secret winning card:

> ***And God helped him against the Philistines, and against the Arabians that dwelt in Gurbaal, and the Mehunims.***

He had a stable government because God helped him against his enemies. That is the same way I believe God is going to help you combat the enemies (barrenness, poverty, confusion, etc.) in your marriage. As help comes to you from heaven, they will all bow to you, in Jesus' name!

God's Involvement In The Family

In the story of creation in Genesis chapter 1, everything God spoke into existence, He saw. But when it came to the issue of marriage, He didn't just speak it into existence; He was practically involved in instituting it.

> ***And the Lord God said, It is not good that the man should be alone; I will make him an help meet for him.***
>
> ***And the Lord God caused a deep sleep to fall upon Adam, and he slept: and he took one of his ribs, and closed up the flesh instead thereof;***
>
> ***And the rib, which the Lord God had taken from man, made he a woman, and brought her unto the man.***
>
> Genesis 2:18, 21-22

Since He is almighty, God could have simply said, "Let there be marriage" or "Let there be family life" and marriage would have been instituted. But the Bible says, *"He took."* Even though it's not explicitly stated, I strongly believe God must have come down physically into the Garden of Eden, to have been able to cause a deep sleep to come upon Adam, and to remove one of his ribs while he was asleep.

Whatever was strong enough to cause God to leave His throne in heaven must be very important. *"He took"*, because something very important was on the way for man. Rather than taking the rib from Adam's side, God could have simply commanded the rib to come out. But He didn't, showing how dear the marriage institution is to God. Therefore, it should be precious to you and me also.

Not only did God take the rib from Adam's side, but He *"made"* a woman out of it, and *"brought"* her to Adam. These are action words that connote God's physical involvement in establishing marriage.

God's whole intention for instituting marriage is to take shame away from the life of man.

> ***And they were both naked, the man and his wife, and were not ashamed.***
>
> Genesis 2:25

God showed His interest in marriage by personally fashioning the woman and delivering her to her husband. It is, therefore, untrue to assume that the union of a man and a woman in marriage is man's idea, or a cultural and traditional affair.

Therefore, to enjoy God's best in your marriage, you must make Him the centre of your home. You must be ready to give Him priority place, recognizing Him as the foundation for a successful marriage.

The problem with many couples is that they push God aside, and yet expect to enjoy divine benefits. They ignore the Word of God, which I call the "manufacturer's manual" and expect the product (marriage) to function perfectly. But it is impossible!

> ***If the foundations be destroyed, what can the righteous do?***
>
> Psalm 11:3

God is the foundation for success in the home. But when the foundation is faulty, no matter how righteous you may be, your home cannot stand. The right place to begin from is a personal relationship with God, through Jesus Christ. Not stopping there, you must be a diligent student of the Word, studying and practising it, as it is what holds the key to an exciting and successful marriage.

So, marital bliss depends on the place you give to God and His Word in your home. The more of Him you have, the more of peace, joy, happiness and sweetness you enjoy in your family.

> ***...Upholding all things by the word of his power...***
>
> Hebrews 1:3

All things, including marriage, are upheld by the Word of God. God is power, and He upholds all things, including your home, by His powerful Word. Once God's Word is given its rightful place in your home, it is built on a sure foundation, which must stand! Receive the grace to operate upon the Word now, in Jesus' name!

I heard of the testimony of a sister who was quite advanced in age, already above 40 years and yet was not married. She encountered God's Word in Isaiah 60:9,

> ***Surely the isles shall wait for me, and the ships of Tarshish first, to bring thy sons from far, their silver and their gold with them, unto the name of the LORD thy God, and to the Holy One of Israel, because he hath glorified thee.***

She decided that she was going to patiently wait on God to bring His son (her husband) from far with silver and gold, as she committedly glorified God by service in church.

Not too long after this encounter, God spoke to a very handsome, rich brother in another branch of the same church to relocate to this sister's branch. It was while there God showed him this sister as his future wife. They are not only married now, but are blessed with children.

God's Word never fails. You can depend on it to bring

your desires to pass, if you will be committed to pay the price to locate it as it applies to you.

Three

Satan's Interest In The Home

– David

God's plan for the family is revealed in Genesis 2:18:

> ***And the Lord God said, It is not good that the man should be alone; I will make him an help meet for him.***

He established marriage for the purpose of making life good for man. After He instituted marriage, God confirmed that it was very good. However, it was not long after that the enemy arrived on the scene. As a matter of fact, it was soon after God performed the wedding ceremony, and declared, "Behold Mr. and Mrs. Adam", that Satan showed up.

Satan is the enemy of everything good. Having lost access to goodness immediately he fell from heaven, he cannot stand anyone else enjoying good. He is envious of any good thing, so he goes about reversing the order of things. This is what makes him wicked.

People attribute the crisis in homes to incompatibility or disagreements, but it is actually Satan who is behind the woes in families. He has determined to cause havoc in homes. He would do anything or pay any price to shatter a home. Quite a number, even in the Church, are victims of this satanic onslaught against families.

Some wish they were never married, yet God says, "I created it for your good." I can imagine Adam wishing he was never created, when he was driven out of Eden into the wilderness. I picture him running away from the wild animals which had been his pets before Satan entered the garden and sent man out.

I perceive that Satan was envious of the fact that the couple were standing on their feet, while he was crawling on the ground. So he came with a mission to have them grounded. But the good news is that although Satan bruised the heel of mankind, to floor him, man can bruise his head and wound him fatally. This was what Jesus came to do on earth. As the seed of the woman, His mission on earth was to bruise Satan's head and empower us to do the same.

> ***And I will put enmity between thee and the woman, and between thy seed and her seed; it shall bruise thy head, and thou shalt bruise his heel.***
>
> Genesis 3:15

> ***Behold, I give unto you power to tread on serpents and scorpions, and over all the power of the enemy: and nothing shall by any means hurt you.***
>
> Luke 10:19

To counteract the activity of Satan against the family unit, Jesus' first miracle was at a wedding ceremony in Cana of Galilee (John 2). Whereas the first thing Satan did was to destroy a family, the first miracle Jesus performed was to wipe away shame from a family.

Jesus summarizes the situation and His mission on earth very clearly in John 10:10:

> ***The thief cometh not, but for to steal, and to kill, and to destroy: I am come that they might have life, and that they might have it more abundantly.***

Satan's mission of stealing, killing and destroying is first targeted at the home. His primary concern is how to steal the joy, peace and love that exist between couples. All his plan is on how to move the man against the woman, so that one of them would eventually move out of their home, the same way he drove Adam and Eve out of Eden. He still prowls around looking for gullible people to drive away from their homes.

That is why you suddenly find a couple who, just a few minutes ago, were calling each other "Sweety" or "Honey", pouncing on each other as bulls in a fight. The sweetness in their home turns sour, until it becomes so bitter that there is no trace of sweetness in it again. Perhaps if the husband used to call his wife "Honey", Satan comes in and moves him to say to her, "If this marriage wants to break, let it break. After all, marriage is not the Kingdom of God." All Satan wants is to destroy the union, by destroying the things that join them together.

That is why Jesus said, *"I am come that they might have life, and that they might have it more abundantly."* That life abundant is first directed to the homes.

Satan hangs around beautiful things so he can corrupt the beauty. He hung around Job, because his life was beautiful. He continued till he destroyed the beauty around Job. Satan has not changed his techniques. Once he sees an ever joyful couple, he says, "I must get them." He hates to see any family successful, and he would stop at nothing to destroy it.

Every family is vulnerable to Satan's attacks. He still goes about to and fro as a roaring lion, seeking families to devour. However, it is within your power to oppose him.

One of the enemy's trump cards against the home is polygamy, particularly in Africa. He deceives a man into marrying another wife under the excuse that the first is not living up to expectation. So, the man takes a second, a third, and even a fourth wife, because he soon discovers that the subsequent wives are worse than the first.

Satan is a trickster! He has no power, only tricks. Right from Eden, he had no strength, but tricks. When you are unaware of his devices, he takes advantage of your ignorance to buffet you. He is still looking for families to push out of their gardens of Eden today. His method is still the same. He questions God's instructions and challenges everything God says. He still whispers to husbands, "Has God said, 'Thou shalt love thy wife as Christ loved the Church?' But can you call that woman a wife? She's a witch! God said you should love your wife, not a witch..."

Then he goes to the woman and says, "Has God actually said, 'Thou shalt submit to your husband in everything'? No, not when it's obviously a stupid thing to do. Remember that the reason you went to school is to be able to reason out issues!"

Satan fights absolute statements. All he wants is to

get you to eat the "forbidden fruit" of hatred, pride, selfishness, etc. But you won't eat it, in Jesus' name! Even if your husband is an unbeliever (you probably got married before you were born again), God's Word says you can win him to Jesus without speaking a word, by your life-style (1 Peter 3:1-2).

Satan may have suggested to you that even though God says you should submit to your husband, He doesn't mean to an unbeliever. But know that even if he is an unbeliever, except he departs on his own volition, you must remain in the union (1 Corinthians 7:12-15).

Satan Looks For Loopholes

> ***But I fear, lest by any means, as the serpent beguiled Eve through his subtilty, so your minds should be corrupted from the simplicity that is in Christ.***
>
> 2 Corinthians 11:3

Every successful home is a threat to Satan's kingdom; that's why he would do anything to destroy it. Unfortunately, he gains entrance to many homes often through the woman. Remember he gained access into the first home through Eve, and history always repeats itself.

For this reason, men should protect their wives spiritually, to ensure that they do not engage in private discussions with hell, which can send them out of their "garden." Once the woman is effectively shielded from Satan, he will have difficulty in trying to penetrate the home.

Women are more susceptible to the attacks of Satan because of their roles in the home. She is usually more at home than the man, so is more available to Satan. He creeps in on her and tells her, "What makes you different from the man? Are you a slave? Have you forgotten that you are also educated as he (husband) is? Have you forgotten your placement in your office? There is neither Jew nor Greek, male or female; the same Lord is rich unto all." If unguarded, the woman would be tempted to agree with him.

Somehow, Satan is able to easily secure the attention of women, particularly when they are idle. He barrages them with all sorts of negative information, which in turn makes them unhappy. He often arrests them by painting a deadly picture of calamity and woe, which they readily accept. But unfortunately, some women claim that it was God that revealed such information to them, not recognizing that it came through "the prince of the power of the air."

Woman, please learn to prove the source of the information that comes to you. Find things out for yourself from the Word of God, because nothing anybody says can make the Word of no effect. The destruction many families have experienced today came from information that had satanic sources.

Man, it's time to be awake and chase Satan out of your garden! Until you say, "Get thee behind this family, Satan," he will keep hanging around.

Why Satan Wants Your Home

To Stop You From Destroying His Kingdom

> ***How should one chase a thousand, and two put ten thousand to flight, except their Rock had sold them, and the Lord had shut them up?***
>
> Deuteronomy 32:30

As man's eternal enemy, Satan has vowed to pull down the family unit. But why? Whereas in the covenant one can deal with 1,000, two, especially in marriage, are empowered to put 10,000 to flight! Satan knows this and wants to keep his kingdom, so he launches attacks on the family, to prevent them from destroying his kingdom. Since one family can destroy 1,000 demons, Satan aims at destroying the 10,000 capacity destroyers. If he succeeds, he has preserved more demons to run errands for him.

To Hinder Your Prayer

Another reason the devil wants to gain entrance into

families is found in 1 Peter 3:7:

> ***Likewise, ye husbands, dwell with them according to knowledge, giving honour unto the wife, as unto the weaker vessel, and as being heirs together of the grace of life; that your prayers be not hindered.***

When a man and his wife are at variance with each other, their prayers are hindered, and they are disconnected from God. They may pray all the time, but there will be no response from heaven. Heaven will be shut, making it impossible for them to enjoy the harvest of whatever seed they may have sown.

The man who opens up his home to malice or discord has blocked his access to God's blessing. Satan knows this, so he does all he can to see that there is rancour and strife between a man and his wife. Anytime you sense any animosity rising within you against your spouse, know that Satan is seeking an entrance. Therefore, resist him steadfastly in the faith. Tell yourself that since you have no intention of having another home, you will not give Satan a foothold in your family.

Four

Instituted for Dominion

– David

> ***And God said, Let us make man in our image, after our likeness: and let them have dominion over the fish of the sea, and over the fowls of the air, and over the cattle, and over all the earth, and over every creeping thing that creepeth upon the earth.***
>
> Genesis 1:26

Marriage is not an association founded by men, but an institution established by God. He instituted marriage for earthly dominion. Any family that genuinely stays together in the marriage covenant is bound to enjoy dominion in all areas of life.

The Key Of Agreement

To enjoy all-round family dominion, however, husband and wife must always be in agreement, as it is the key that unlocks the door to family dominion. Disagreement between husband and wife shuts the door to family dominion.

> ***How should one chase a thousand, and two put ten thousand to flight, except their Rock had sold them, and the Lord had shut them up?***
>
> Deuteronomy 32:30

> ***Again I say unto you, That if two of you shall agree on earth as touching any thing that they shall ask, it shall be done for them of my Father which is in heaven.***
>
> Matthew 18:19

This is the mystery behind dominion in the family. It is the point where you agree as touching anything on earth and it is done for you by your Father in heaven. The root of dominion is found in marriage; therefore, people who know how to operate the covenant of marriage enjoy dominion. Ecclesiastes 4:9-10 says:

> ***Two are better than one; because they have a good reward for their labour.***

For if they fall, the one will lift up his fellow: but woe to him that is alone when he falleth; for he hath not another to help him up.

Any man who is alone can easily be overcome. That is why in marriage, husband and wife become one; and as one, they are able to exercise dominion over all situations of life. By the marriage union, they enter into the strongest human agreement, and are able to accomplish whatever they desire.

The struggles and ultimate failure experienced in many families today are traceable to a lack of agreement in the home. The devil takes special delight in breaking down agreement in the home, because he knows that once disagreement has crept in between a couple, their dominion is at stake.

My wife and I are always in agreement, so there is no way the devil can come between us or into our home. Since we are in agreement, we enjoy dominion over sickness, financial difficulties, etc. I remember showing my wife what the Bible says in Genesis 2:18: ***And the Lord God said, It is not good that the man should be alone; I will make him an help meet for him.*** She is, in essence, an help meet for me. She agreed with me, and we have not had the first argument to date!

Someone else may share the same Scripture with his

wife, but if she chooses to agree with the old wives' tales of her grandparents instead, and despise her husband's counsel, problems will arise in the home.

That is why I believe that the problems in many marriages are due mainly to a lack of covenant agreement. Many people agree with culture, at the expense of the covenant agreement they should have in the home. Amos 3:3 asks:

Can two walk together, except they be agreed?

Marriage is meant for agreement, not for disagreement. Until husband and wife are in agreement, family dominion will be impossible. Look at this testimony:

"On December 14, 1994, I lost my first son (who was a year and seven months old) when I went to deliver my second baby. My house help kept kerosine in an ice cream cup, which the boy drank. He was taken to the hospital, but died the following day. I wasn't informed, because I had just put to bed.

On January 6, 1995, my husband's family said I was the one that killed my son. They told my husband to pack out of the house, so he left me and the new baby, packing all his belongings.

On January 8, 1995, a friend of mine brought me to this glorious church, where God Himself dwells. Since

I came here, I can see the hand of God in my family, as He has given me rest round-about.

In the month of February, the Bishop taught on the importance of the Blood of Jesus, and said that we should plead it on our environment. Also, he made a prophetic utterance, that after the service, those we were looking for would look for us. I caught this word, because I had been going to beg my husband to come back home.

When I got home after the service, the gateman told me that oga had come looking for me twice. He came back in the night, and told me that he was coming back the next day, and he did! We are now living in peace and harmony!" – **Eyesan, N.**

Know that your wife won't plan your hurt neither would your husband want to harm you. The devil is behind the strife in your home. He is hanging around, in an attempt to destroy your covenant dominion in Christ. But you can choose not to give him any room. My wife knows that I will never do anything to hurt her and I know she won't deliberately try to hurt me, so there is no strife between us.

If your wife puts too much salt in the soup, for instance, see it as a result of her attempt to ensure that there is enough salt in the soup, not that she did it deliberately.

A brother in Kaduna decided to put an end to a five-year strife between himself and his wife. During those years they lived in strife, their home was nothing but a hostel. But as soon as he resolved the difference, those who had owed him for many years paid him that same week! Disagreement stole the family's financial dominion.

It is time to grow up. You cannot afford to be a boy in understanding. You need to earnestly desire an increase in understanding, because it is what enables you to walk successfully in the covenant of marriage.

> ***Brethren, be not children in understanding: howbeit in malice be ye children, but in understanding be men.***
>
> 1 Corinthians 14:20

Once there is agreement in the three dimensions of a man's life (spirit, soul and body), the couple have in their hands one of the greatest and most potent forces. Agreement in the body entails not being committed to any other person physically, but your spouse. In the realm of the mind, you should share the same thoughts, imaginations, dreams and aspirations. Just as it was in Genesis 11:6, a husband and wife can also be totally united, believing in the same things and sharing a unity of faith.

It is time couples resolved whatever differences exist between them, otherwise they will lose their dominion. If both parties will only purpose to be in total agreement on all issues concerning their home, it will be impossible for barrenness, financial difficulties, etc, to have access to them.

Couples must be in total covenant agreement. For instance, if I tell my wife today that the Lord is sending me to T'Chad, there will be no need to persuade her. She knows that I won't say such a thing for the fun of it, or for lack of anything to say. The covenant between us forbids that. Men, there is a need for maturity, so that your leadership position can be enhanced spiritually.

One of the ways agreement can be enhanced in a home is when the man gives vision and direction to his wife. If your wife knows where you are headed for per time, she will learn to trust you and your sense of judgment and be able to willingly agree with you per time. That perhaps has been one of the things that have enhanced the agreement in my home. My wife, ever before we got married, knew my passion and zeal for God and that knowledge has propelled her to do all within her power to ensure I have her cooperation on all fronts.

I remember once the Lord told me to drop my wife's entire salary as an offering. As her custom is, she brought the salary to me and I told her what the Lord had told me. She only said, "Praise the Lord." She neither argued nor tried to talk me out of obeying God. In a matter of a few days, the testimony of that sacrifice began to speak.

For some couples, this could have degenerated into a huge argument that would have denied them of the breakthrough they so badly desire.

Remember that marriage is the strongest human covenant, and those who know how to operate it enjoy dominion in all areas of life.

Five

For Good, Better And Best

- Faith

> ***And the Lord God said, It is not good that the man should be alone; I will make him an help meet for him.***
>
> Genesis 2:18

Marriage is not a trap. It was instituted for the good of man. Marriage was designed to make life great for mankind. In the beginning, God saw that it is not good for man to be alone, so He instituted marriage. I believe God must have said to Himself, "I want it to be good for man, so I will make him a help meet for him."

We understand that every good and perfect gift comes

from the Father of lights (James 1:17). Therefore, marriage should make a man move up on the ladder of progress. It should take him from good to better, from better to best, and from best to the point of perfection in life. There is always a place called forward, which you must strive to get to (Exodus 14:15).

But many are scared of entering into marriage, because they see it as an instrument of stagnation. Marriage is meant to advance, increase and promote one. It is not a necessary evil, as you may have heard and probably believed. Rather, it is designed to make life complete for you. A bachelor may say, "But life is good for me now." But no matter the kind of wonderful experience you may be having now, the Bible says:

> ***Two are better than one; because they have a good reward for their labour.***
>
> ***For if they fall, the one will lift up his fellow: but woe to him that is alone when he falleth; for he hath not another to help him up.***
>
> ***Again, if two lie together, then they have heat: but how can one be warm alone?***
>
> ***And if one prevail against him, two shall withstand him...***
>
> Ecclesiastes 4:9-12

Marriage provides you an opportunity for better living!

I used to be scared by certain marriage vows I hear couples chant on their wedding day. They say such things as: "I so and so get into wedlock with you, for better for worse, for richer for poorer, in sickness and in health..." I saw the ignorance of the officiating Priest and the intending couples as they chant the so-called marriage vows, because marriage is not designed to be "for better for worse", but "for better for best!"

As far as God is concerned, marriage is for better living. That is why Deuteronomy 32:30 says:

> ***How should one chase a thousand, and two put ten thousand to flight?***

Jesus reiterated this below:

> ***Again I say unto you, That if two of you shall agree on earth as touching any thing that they shall ask, it shall be done for them of my Father which is in heaven.***
>
> Matthew 18:19

This must be why God instructs husbands to dwell with their wives according to knowledge, so that their prayers be not hindered (1 Peter 3:7). Marriage provides a covenant platform for efficacious prayer. Whatever a couple agrees upon in prayer is done for them.

Marriage gives you access to double victory, as a couple can put ten thousand to flight. Also, when one party is cold, the other is available to warm him or her up. When one is down, the other will lift him or her up. The ultimate in marriage is for the best in life, and you will get there. God never made provision for your life condition to be worse after marriage, so, why expect and express it?

For Better Living

Marriage was instituted for better living for mankind. It is not to bring hurts or constitute a hindrance. The Amplified Version of the Bible renders Genesis 2:18 this way:

> ***Now the Lord God said, It is not good (sufficient, satisfactory) that the man should be alone; I will make him a helper meet (suitable, adapted, complementary) for him.***

The kind of help God intended marriage to provide is one that is suitable, adaptable and complementary; it is expected to cover all areas of life.

Spiritually

Spiritually, God expects you to be a positive influence on your spouse, so that you can both press on to greater spiritual heights.

A man who does not care about the spiritual state of

his wife is not helping her. Perhaps he discovers that her spiritual life is not what it used to or should be. Probably, she is weak in prayer, in studying the Word and other spiritual matters. He shouldn't just fold his hands unconcerned, watching her life deteriorate. Such a husband is not a help-meet.

A husband who, rather than help his wife to stay spiritually vibrant, concentrates on himself alone is selfish. He should know that at the end of the day, what will happen can be likened to the effect of the force of gravity on an object that is thrown up. Very soon, the object will stop going up and start coming down. A wife who is spiritually weak can pull down her spiritual-giant of a husband, and vice versa.

So, as you strive to grow in the things of God, make sure you go along with your spouse. That way, two will be better than one, because they are both working towards the same spiritual goal.

Socially

God expects couples to also help one another socially. For instance, due to your partner's background, he or she may not know certain social manners, such as table manners, matching colours, appropriate dressing codes for various occasions, etc. It is your responsibility to educate your spouse on them.

The essence of marriage is for couples to help each other.

Financially

God expects a husband and wife to be financially transparent to one another. They should not keep things away from each other, especially when it concerns money matters.

In some cultures, the men believe that it is a shameful thing for their wives to know how much they earn. But the truth is, if you hide your earning from your wife, she will definitely make demands that are beyond your means, as she doesn't know how much you earn. You have to make up your mind whether to hold on to culture or to hold on to the Word of God.

Some women also believe that their husbands alone are responsible for providing for the home. They will even quote Scriptures to back up this belief. No wonder, when such women earn their own money, they hide it from their husbands, and make them pay for everything in the home.

Wife, don't keep your money for the purpose of buying the latest clothes, shoes and headgear in town only. You make yourself look like a prostitute when you give your husband your body, but cannot give him your money.

Couples are expected to help each other in every area of life. They are expected to give succour to each other. Be honest with one another, so that your marriage can last. Remember that whatever money you have belongs to both of you. Money has put many homes asunder, don't let it put yours asunder.

Mentally

Adam wasn't created a dunce. He was created an intelligent being. How else could he have given names to all the animals in the garden of Eden, if his mind was not active and alive? The names he gave to those animals are what they still bear today. 1 Corinthians 2:16 tells us: ***...But we have the mind of Christ.***

God created you with a sound mind. So, in marriage, both the man and the woman are supposed to be mentally sound and alive. Marriage is meant to improve you mentally. The Scripture says two are better than one. So, when a sound mind comes in contact with another sound mind in marriage, the two of them will enter a better realm of living.

Before taking decisions about the home, a husband and wife should first reason things out together. They place facts side by side, considering the benefits and the deficits before taking a decision. That way, they will be able to take better decisions.

To enable us take better decisions on certain family issues, my husband and I spend time to reason out things with God. For instance, we usually reason out issues that concern the education of our children, considering the advantages and disadvantages. Remember that even God says we should come and reason together (Isaiah 1:18). That way, we have been able to strike a balance between their spiritual and academic life.

Physically

Also, husband and wife are expected to be helpers of one another physically. Husband, your wife will definitely sometimes require your masculine attributes to help her get some physical tasks accomplished. May be you are moving to a new apartment, and there are some heavy items to be moved. Your wife needs your muscles at such times. Do not absent yourself at such times, in the name of being busy in the office. Be available to help her.

Wife, there will be times when your husband will need your feminine nature to get things done. For example, he may need you to help massage his legs, back or body after a very busy day at work. Don't claim to be very busy in the kitchen or with the children. Please be available. Somebody once said, "Men are boys in trousers." Remember, marriage is meant for better living.

Six

Getting Into Marriage

- David

Marriage is not a myth, neither is it magic. Marriage is a relationship that is to be consciously entered into. You don't wake up one morning and find somebody by your side. That last happened in the Garden of Eden. After the incident in the Garden of Eden, God's new rule for marriage is:

> ***Whoso findeth a wife findeth a good thing, and obtaineth favour of the Lord.***
>
> Proverbs 18:22

"Whoso findeth..." not, "Whoso prayeth...", "Whoso fasteth", or "Whoso his father or mother giveth a wife."

Every man must find his wife, and the finding is not a spiritual process. You must open your physical eyes wide in order to find. That way, you are able to assess what you are seeing, whether it is what you really want or not.

In this chapter, I will be discussing seven steps to getting into marriage. They are steps I also went through, when I was getting into marriage. To get the best in anything, you need facts, which I consider as the father of success. The steps are — Propose, Prepare, Proceed, Promote, Protect, Protest and Possess. They will help you make an intelligent decision on who to marry.

Propose

The journey into marriage begins with a proposal. It requires your walking up to the lady you have chosen to marry (out of the many you saw), and telling her that you want to marry her. You shouldn't beat around the bush or harass her when telling her you want to marry her. All you need do is go straight to the point and tell her your intentions. You may say to her, "I want your hand in marriage. Think about it and let me know your decision." Don't go telling a lady, "God said you are my wife." Each one shall find his own wife, and by himself.

Your proposal must be as a result of your choice, which was based on facts. Don't allow religion to cloud your decision on who to marry. What should inform your choice of who to marry is, "Do I agree with her personality, style and outlook?" Amos 3:3 says:

Can two walk together, except they be agreed?

Your decision on who to marry should not be based on dreams either. A marriage proposal must be based on articulated facts, such as, "Do we have the same goals?" "Are we going in the same direction?" God respects your choice, so don't be afraid to make one.

However, it is not only the man that has a right to make choices; the woman also has a right to decide who she wants to marry. So, don't put pressure on people to marry you, neither should you gather people around an innocent lady, to put pressure on her to agree to marry you.

Also, when trying to decide who to marry, never choose to marry an unbeliever, no matter the vision, dream or counsel. The Abrahamic covenant demands that you marry among your kinsmen only. As a believer, your kinsman is a fellow believer. You are not permitted to marry a stranger. Do not ever think that someday she might be saved. It is easier for an unbeliever to make you backslide, than for you to save her. 2 Corinthians 6:14-16 commands:

> ***Be ye not unequally yoked together with unbelievers: for what fellowship hath righteousness with unrighteousness? and what communion hath light with darkness?***
>
> ***And what concord hath Christ with Belial? or what part hath he that believeth with an infidel?***
>
> ***And what agreement hath the temple of God with idols? for ye are the temple of the living God...***

The unbeliever is definitely out of the way when considering who to marry. You don't even need to pray about it.

Proposal should be based on facts, and when the response from the other party is positive, then preparation begins.

Prepare

This is a fact-finding period, when the man and lady start getting to know themselves and begin to put their facts together into the future they both anticipate. If at this stage the relationship is not going on well, or you discover that you can't go any further because you both disagree on ideas, and that your expectations are miles apart, then common sense demands that you call it quits immediately.

Breaking an engagement is scripturally permitted; it is not considered as a divorce and should not be mistaken for one. Saying "Yes" to a marriage proposal is different from saying "Yes" in actual marriage. Many tolerate themselves during their engagement period and eventually get married, and thereafter enter into crisis.

The quality of preparation you put into any given task determines the quality of result you get from it. Lack of adequate preparation is the reason for the high rate of divorce in America and the rest of the western world. They marry very quickly and pack it up just as fast too.

A period of preparation is allowed in the African culture. But unfortunately, when once you are engaged in Africa, marriage is in most cases mandatory. Once both families get to know themselves, an attempt to call off the relationship is often resisted by members of either family. Some families would say they have already accepted kolanuts (a traditional symbol of acceptance in marriage) from the other family, so it is impossible to break the relationship. Young men and women, please don't allow anybody to tie your destiny down with simple kolanut.

The preparation for marriage is not just in prayers,

but in fact-finding and in an intelligent analysis of available facts, to determine whether there is any future in the decision to marry. My preparation for marriage took six years, but its effect is speaking now. My wife knew all about what I was doing when we were in courtship, so she knew what to expect in future.

Once your preparation is satisfactory, you move on to the next step.

Proceed

It is at this stage you proceed to inform all those who need to be informed, such as both parents and family members. You are not permitted to proceed until you are satisfied with the available facts.

Promote

At this point, you start promoting the plan for marriage. You begin to take practical steps towards getting married by putting the necessary things for marriage in place.

For instance, as a man, you can't be a squatter and want to be married. This period of promoting the relationship is, therefore, the time to secure an apartment, no matter the size. If three of you were sharing a flat before you got married, things can't continue like that after marriage, otherwise, what you will have would be a slave, not a wife. She will have to do all the cooking and laundry for both you and all the young men in the house.

Also, as long as you are living in your father's or uncle's boys' quarters, you are still a boy. One room outside your uncle's house makes a home, unlike a boys' quarters behind his house. So, a man that wants to marry must have a place where he can be a man, not where he is still considered as a boy.

You are not qualified for marriage if you are still eating your father's food. If you don't have a room, a bed and cooking pots, then you are not qualified for marriage. Age is not what determines your preparedness for marriage. What you have not prepared for, you can't succeed in.

Protect

Now that you are set for marriage, you must protect your destiny by protecting yourselves from defilement. The honour in marriage must be preserved by preserving the marriage bed from defilement.

> ***Marriage is honourable in all, and the bed undefiled: but whoremongers and adulterers God will judge.***
>
> Hebrews 13:4

Marriage is honourable, as long as the bed is not defiled. Defilement of the bed is the defilement of marital destiny. It takes the mercy of God to restore the honour in marriage once it is defiled.

Temptation is not equal to sin. Falling into temptation is what is termed sin. Jesus was tempted at all points, just as we are, yet He was without sin. You take cover under God in prayers and then take practical steps to protect yourself from falling. Protection is very crucial to your desired future.

Protest

This is the time to say "no" to any unpleasant or unacceptable issue you may have discovered in each other. If you can't understand yourselves well before you get married and start living together, you will never have an outstanding family. You need to know what goes well with one another, and courtship period is the time to do it.

For instance, if you had earlier agreed on certain terms and then suddenly there is a deviation from it, you are allowed to react. This protest will help put the issues right, so that when the home is eventually established, there will be freedom and a free flow of communication between you.

Also, if any of your partner's family members raise some issues that can jeopardize your future, you are permitted to protest. You have the right to say, "This won't work, on so and so basis."

When I was about to marry, certain things were included on the list of things I was to bring as the bride price. I knew I couldn't take those things there. I would rather never be married than present those things, because of my stand for God and my future. I knew I loved my wife to be and that we were looking forward to getting married, but I loved my God more.

When I got the list, I didn't respond. Then one day, my in-laws said to me, "We sent so and so paper to you and you didn't respond." God gave me wisdom to reply them, and I said, "You see, there were certain things on the list, that if we get involved in them now, we would become problems to you tomorrow." My father-in-law agreed with me and said, "Cancel whatever is against your future on the list."

You can't be a boy and succeed in marriage. You must be a man with respectable opinions. But if people have to buy wedding suit and shirts for you, then they will have the final say in your marital affairs.

Possess

After all the above is accomplished, the next thing to

do is to possess your husband or wife, and then the home is born. This is the point where you both march to the altar to be wedded. It is at this point that the young man can now stand in front of many witnesses and say, "I, Victor... I, Samuel... wed thee."

At this stage, the man is set for his home. He is set mentally; he is satisfied with everything about the lady. Physically, he is in order, and the system to make the home succeed is in place. He is leaving boyhood for manhood, as marriage is not for boys, but only for men.

At this point, you can be sure that a great future awaits you in your home, and that you are heading for something very colourful and glorious. The race is not permitted to begin until after these steps are satisfactorily in place. If you are absolutely responsible for your choice, then you won't look for someone to blame.

You will not fail! Your home shall be the haven God created it to be, in Jesus' name!

Seven

The Law Of Departure

- David

> ***...For this cause shall a man leave father and mother, and shall cleave to his wife: and they twain shall be one flesh?***
>
> ***Wherefore they are no more twain, but one flesh. What therefore God hath joined together, let not man put asunder.***
>
> Matthew 19:5-6

The source of troubles in many Christian homes today, is the failure to do the point I am about to discuss in this chapter. Incidentally also, it is one of the seven concepts of marriage God revealed to me. I call it the law of departure. When this law is broken, you automatically open the door to all manner of negative events.

There is nothing more devastating in marriage than for either partner in marriage to be tied to the apron strings of his or her parents. For every small decision to be taken in the home, he or she says, "I am going home", because he never left home in the first place. A boy can't leave home, only men can. Neither can a girl leave home, only a woman can. That's why many couples are in a house, but are not at home. Instead, they are at home with their parents.

You must free yourself from the apron strings of your parents before marriage. Matthew 19:5 says:

> ***...For this cause shall a man leave father and mother, and shall cleave to his wife: and they twain shall be one flesh?***

The law of departure is about gaining parental independence before marriage. This does not mean that you have nothing to do with them anymore. Rather, it means your ability to take decisions, independent of your parents, and accepting responsibility for such decisions.

There must be a total departure from parents and friends before there can be a total cleaving of husband

and wife. Some parents, although Christians, still carry over from their unbelieving days, the mentality of perpetual interference in their married children's affairs. They see their sons and daughters as babies, and so cannot trust them to make their own decisions. They, therefore, hang around, to teleguide them as they used to do when the children were in primary school. Parents, let your sons depart, so they can cleave to their wives and enjoy the best of life!

Some other married people can hardly take any decision without first consulting with their parents. They cannot be said to be men, but boys! Marriage is for men and women, not for boys and girls!

At the slightest provocation, some women would say to their husbands, "I am going home." Home? Where is home? This shows their lack of understanding of the covenant of marriage. Until the door is shut against every form of interference in the home, you cannot get the best out of marriage.

When some men want to buy a new car for their wives, they first solicit the opinion of their fathers. "I am thinking of getting a new car for my wife. I just thought I should mention it to you," he says. The old man keeps quiet for a few minutes, and then responds, "Your elder brother does not have a car, and you want to buy a new car for your wife? If I am your father, then listen to me! If you buy that car for her, it will be burnt!" It is not the father's fault, but that of the son, because he has not yet understood the law of departure.

My wife and I are absolutely responsible for all the decisions that affect us. Everyone else only gets to know the end result. If I want to buy something for my wife, I won't need to first consult anyone, for their approval. I don't owe anybody any explanations for decisions concerning my home.

It is time for couples to exhibit some level of maturity. For instance, it is simply a display of immaturity for a man who does not have even a room of his own in his village to gather his entire family and say, "We are going home for Christmas." When they arrive there, little children are chased from their rooms, for the "old babies" from town to have a place to stay. To worsen matters, he arrives there and does not give them any money for food! Yet he, his wife and their eight children eat three square meals daily! Of course, this gives members of his extended family room to control him. That is contrary to the law of departure!

Some aspects of the African culture have created a system of "rescue" for lazy people. They are backward ideas, which make babies of men at seventy! That is the reason why there are few genuine covenant marriages in this part of the world, as undue room is given to interferences from the extended members of the family.

As Christian parents, our part is to trust the Holy Spirit to guide our children in the right choice of a marriage partner. Once they are mature enough and ripe for marriage, allow them to choose their partners as led by the spirit of God. Otherwise, you may later come to hear statements like, "My father really hurt me, he misled me", from them. That won't be your experience in Jesus' name.

There is no point in hurrying your son to get married. Let him become a man first, then you will also have peace. Don't keep telling him, "All your equals are married." That is unnecessary. A lot of my mates married before me, but I told myself that I wasn't walking by their own time-table. I am not running by their programme, but by the one God has revealed to me. God has a perfect plan for everyone of His children (Jer. 29:11) and His ways (plans) are superior to ours any day (Isaiah 55:8-9).

A situation where everyone is put in a tight corner because one child wants to marry, is not right. This uncle is to buy the shoes, another uncle the shirt, a cousin the suit. Who will buy the food after the wedding?

You have to allow your sons become men, and your daughters, women, so they will have a great tomorrow.

I believe very strongly that one reason for the upsurge in the divorce rate in the West is because very many teenagers who met themselves only last week on the football field, are going to court today to be married. Their minds are not mature enough for the responsibility of decision making, so the marriage breaks up. While maturity is not a function of age alone, it does have a vital part to play in any successful marriage.

Cleave to Your Partner

The ultimate aim of the law of departure is so *"they twain shall become one flesh."* Leaving (your parents) should culminate in your cleaving (to your marriage partner). When you have departed from all forms of interferences, you are expected to cleave to your wife or husband, and the two of you become one flesh.

Departure without the husband and wife cleaving to each other will ultimately end up in loneliness and frustration. However, there can be no cleaving except the law of departure is first in place. Ephesians 5:31-32 says:

> ***For this cause shall a man leave his father and mother, and shall be joined unto his wife, and they***

two shall be one flesh.

This is a great mystery: but I speak concerning Christ and the church.

So, we have this great mystery of two becoming one flesh. When this happens, they can ask for anything from heaven and it shall be done for them (Matthew 18:19). Whatever they bind on earth is bound in heaven, and whatever they loose on earth is loosed in heaven. Therefore, **leave,** so you can **cleave**; and when you do, you are sure of success in your family.

The following testimony is a journey that could have been avoided had the man simply applied the law of leaving and cleaving. But thank God, there is a God of a second chance, who can restore peace and joy in any home and situation.

"I was under serious attacks in 1995, after my marriage broke down. I was downcast, and I lost hope of being alive. This was because I have four little children, without any job or house to live in. I was almost going mad.

My husband and his relations had told me to leave Makurdi or that they would kill me and my children. This was because my husband's new wife had said she didn't want to see me in Benue State anymore.

So they started attacking me physically and spiritually.

I was heart-broken and oppressed all-round.

When I went to churches for prayer and counselling, he would tell the pastors to drive me away. Where I was to get an accommodation, he would tell the landlord to reject me. I was totally confused and all my friends abandoned me. It was terrible for my children and me.

In 1995, I felt sick. I could no longer understand anything, I could not walk and there was a big stone in my chest which made it impossible for me to stand erect.

I took medications, but there was no relief. That was when it dawned on me that I was dying. I started crying all night, thinking of what would happen to my little children.

On February 1996, a neighbour came to greet me. When she was leaving, she gave me a handbill of a seminar in Living Faith Church. I determined to go there, even if I had to crawl.

On that day, I pleaded with a neighbour to help me organize a motorcyclist to convey me to the church. Immediately I got to the church premises, and stepped my feet on the ground, the stony heart dropped!

The load was no longer there. So, I could walk on my own into the church. As I walked in, they were singing praises and I too stood up through the praise time, glorifying God.

When the service was over, I went home without any help from anyone again. That ended the sickness in my life, and my children started living a healthy life till today.

I continued worshiping in the church and God began to change my life. I learnt how to stand my ground on the Word. My lost confidence was regained. All the oppositions ceased! The more I dug deeper into the Word, the more things worked for me! God has been fighting for me!

In 1999, a woman, who is my husband's relation came and confessed to me that they actually wanted to kill me, but they could not. She said she wanted to know the type of charm (juju) that I was using. She said since all things were working for me just like that, that she would like to go to the church with me.

In 2001, my husband sent for my children for the first time. He pleaded with them to forgive him. He told them to help him beg me, because he was too ashamed to face me.

When the children asked him what I actually did to offend him, he said, 'Nothing!' Then he confessed that it was his mother, who told him to drive me away, because I am not from their tribe. So, we all forgave him.

In 2002, he came back and told me that he would take over the payment of our children's school fees. From there, he gave me the car he was using at that time.

Now, we are in peace!"

— Dcns. Blessing I.

Eight

Becoming A "Help Meet"

- Faith

Every woman needs to recognize her biblical position in her husband's life. It is the lack of knowledge in this area that has robbed many homes of honour, dignity and success. Hosea 4:6 says: ***My people are destroyed for lack of knowledge.*** The word "perish" means to be stripped of honour and dignity.

Several homes have today lost honour, because both the husband and the wife are ignorant of their roles. In this chapter, I will be discussing the place God expects the woman to occupy in her husband's life.

The Bible tells us in Genesis 2:18:

And the Lord God said, It is not good that the man should be alone; I will make him an help meet for him.

"Help" means "to give aid and assistance", while *"meet"* means "to surround". Therefore, a *"help meet"* implies one who "surrounds with aid and assistance."

God created the woman for the purpose of surrounding her man with aid and assistance. That is, assisting the man to put in place those things that might be missing in his life.

As his wife, you know things about him that nobody else does. You know him to his closet. You know his nakedness, his down sitting and uprising. You are, however, not to use that against him. Do not use his weaknesses against him, nor despise him for his weaknesses and seek opportunities to disgrace him in the public. Rather, as a help meet, you are to surround him with aid and assistance in those identified weak areas. God wants you to help that man with all the spiritual, emotional and physical aid he requires.

You are meant to complement each other by filling up the vacuum in each others' lives.

There is a pathetic story of Isaac and Rebecca in Genesis 27. Rebecca failed in her duty as Isaac's help meet, and played an unpleasant role in the incidence of Jacob "stealing" Esau's blessing.

Isaac was old and so could not see, because his eyes were dim. Rebecca knew this weakness, but rather than complement him by helping him, she exploited the situation by "assisting" Jacob to steal Esau's blessing.

It was Rebecca that initiated the idea of Jacob stealing Esau's blessing. Even when Jacob noted the loopholes in the plan, Rebecca still convinced Jacob to go ahead. Without her support, Jacob would not have been able to deceive Isaac and steal Esau's blessings. She used her husband's weakness against him and her son.

Woman, have you observed the downward trend in your husband's spiritual life, yet you don't care? Rather than take positive steps, you run him down, tongue-lashing him and patting yourself on the back for being more "spiritual"? By so doing, you are treading on shaky ground, because very soon you will realize that the body cannot move when the head has been knocked off!

Wife, you are meant to be a help that is meet. You are created to surround your man with aid and assistance. His life should be better as a result of his association with you. Your contributions in his life should be positive. If the vices he had before you were married keep increasing rather than decreasing, if his life remains at the same spot, then you are not carrying out your responsibilities in his life.

You are to bring about a positive change in your husband's life. The difference in his life as a result of his marrying you should be glaring for all to see. It is your responsibility to help him attain the great heights God has prepared for him.

Be a helper not a destroyer, an asset not a liability, a blessing not a burden and a soothing balm, not a thorn in the flesh. You know what a thorn does? It makes life uncomfortable and unbearable. It causes a lot of pains. Here is a testimony:

"I have been married for the past ten years, and ever since, there was no peace in the home. For me, marriage wasn't good. Things were just upside down. I had a child in 1993, and it died. I also had series of miscarriages. I used to drive a car, but it was no more. It was as if everything came to a halt.

My husband started coming to Winners' Chapel in January 1997. He didn't ask me to come with him, because I was already attending another Pentecostal church. Yet, there was no peace in the home. The situation worsened, and in June 1997, the tension was so high that I said, 'Lord, what will I do?' I told my husband, 'If this is what marriage is all about, let us call it quit.' He replied, 'Well, the door is wide open. You can go.' It was then I sat down and did a rethink.

I came to Winners' *Chapel in June, and I began to hear the Bishop say, 'I have been married for many years now, and there hasn't been any concern or problem in my home.' I said to myself, 'Is it on this earth or on another planet?'*

But somehow, God has done it for me too! Now I know I had been the problem, not my husband. My husband is a perfect gentleman! The Bishop's wife jokingly says if there was anything as another life, she would still choose to marry her husband. I too can joyfully say the same thing today!" – **Neburabo, R.**

That is what some women are to their husbands — a grief of heart. Instead of assisting the man, they surround him with thorns and thistles. They have made marriage a bed of thorns, instead of roses. If that is what you have been to your husband, stop right now, and ask God to forgive you. It could be the reason you are experiencing calamities, instead of heaven's refreshing in your home. Wherever you have opened the door of your home to the devil through your nonchalance and neglect of wifely duties, ask God to shut that door. He will give you a new beginning and home, if you so desire. Ask God for the grace to constantly surround your husband with aid and assistance.

Give Him His Place

Every man wants his wife to make him feel important. Everyone has an invisible sign hanging from his neck, saying, "Make me feel important." Your husband is no exception. Learn to give your husband his place in the home.

> ***Wives, submit yourselves unto your own husbands, as unto the Lord.***
>
> Ephesians 5:22

Many women are still believing God for the blessing of a home, but God has given you the privilege to be married. He, therefore, expects you to appreciate your man and give him his rightful place in the home. This is another way of surrounding him with aid and assistance.

It can be quite frustrating for a man to have a woman who does not know where God has placed her in the home, and is struggling to take the place of her husband. As a woman, you are not inferior to the man. In God's unique plan, both men and women occupy unique and distinct positions. They are different, but complementary. A woman is uniquely different from her husband. As a matter of fact, she is the crown on her husband's head.

A virtuous woman is a crown to her husband: but she that maketh ashamed is as rottenness in his bones.

Proverbs 12:4

A crown is usually worn on the head. Likewise, a woman or wife is not to be trampled under feet, but to adorn her husband. The husband is the head, and she the ornament of beauty upon his head. The woman is skilfully crafted, so she should be happy and excited about being a woman, and give her husband his God-given place as head in the home.

It is common to find some women who want to take their husband's place as head in the home; they would want to trample their husbands under foot. But such wives will soon be displaced, as they can't take their husband's place, no matter how "beautiful" they are, and their husbands "ugly", or how better educated or from a better family background they may be. They should have married their background then!

The plague of many women is pride, and pride goes before destruction.

Pride goeth before destruction, and an haughty spirit before a fall.

Proverbs 16:18

Pride is the number one destroyer of peace, love, joy

and fulfillment in many homes and marriages today. The Bible says God resists the proud.

> ***...Wherefore he saith, God resisteth the proud, but giveth grace unto the humble.***
>
> James 4:6

Many homes have been destroyed through feminine pride. Woman, that high look, secret pride, arrogant talk and the like must stop, if you desire success in marriage!

> ***These six things doth the Lord hate: yea, seven are an abomination unto him:***
>
> ***A proud look...***
>
> Proverbs 6:16-17

Submission Is The Key

> ***Wives, submit yourselves unto your own husbands, as it is fit in the Lord.***
>
> Colossians 3:18

In the husband-wife relationship, submission is the major key that opens the door to peace, joy, excitement and success in marriage.

Submission can be instrumental in effecting changes in the home, as there is no man that would not respond positively to a submissive wife. A wife's submission to her husband should be absolute. God demands it. You may have been submitting in some things, but not in all, and probably say, "But God knows I am trying my best." But that is not all there is to success in family life. Absolute submission is expected of you.

That may be the missing axe-head that is responsible for the problems in your home. Once you put it in order, your husband will not stop loving you as he used to do when you were in courtship.

> ***Therefore shall a man leave his father and his mother, and shall cleave unto his wife: and they shall be one flesh.***
>
> Genesis 2:24

The word "cleave" originally means to chase. So, when a woman surrounds her husband with aid and assistance, he in turn would not stop loving her. The love between them will keep waxing stronger and stronger.

There is no woman who does not desire to be loved by her husband. But you can only reap a harvest of love, if you sow the seed of submission. I have discovered that the more I stand in my God-ordained place in my husband's life, the more love comes my way from him. But I want more of his love. Everyone close to us knows that my husband loves me. But frankly, I want more love. So, I stand firmly in my place, and keep surrounding him with aid and assistance.

Begin to look out for the areas in your husband's life that require more assistance, and render them willingly and with a pure heart. You will find his love for you getting stronger by the day.

Please say this prayer: "Lord, grant me the grace to constantly surround my husband with aid and assistance, in Jesus' name!"

Nine

Covenant Obligations of Husbands and Wives

- David

The Husband's Obligations

> *For the husband is the head of the wife, even as Christ is the head of the church: and he is the saviour of the body...*
>
> *Husbands, love your wives, even as Christ also loved the church, and gave himself for it;*

That he might sanctify and cleanse it with the washing of water by the word,

That he might present it to himself a glorious church, not having spot, or wrinkle, or any such thing; but that it should be holy and without blemish.

So ought men to love their wives as their own bodies. He that loveth his wife loveth himself.

For no man ever yet hated his own flesh; but nourisheth and cherisheth it, even as the Lord the church...

Nevertheless let every one of you in particular so love his wife even as himself; and the wife see that she reverence her husband.

Ephesians 5:23-33

The man is the principal figure in the family unit. God reckons with his position as head of the home and holds him responsible for any mishap that occurs in it. For instance, when things went wrong in the Garden of Eden, God did not question the woman. Rather, Adam was the one held responsible (Genesis 3:9).

The man is the principal actor in every home. Until the husband accepts his responsibility as head, there can be nothing like success in that family. I am not referring only to men who are married to Christian wives, but also to those who are married to unbelieving ones (they probably got married before they got born again).

If the men accept God's instructions and do them, their homes will be very successful.

But what is the master key to making the home successful?

Love

The Love responsibility is the master key. Love is the instrument a man uses to make his wife a glorious woman, without spot or wrinkle, or any such thing. Therefore, the making of any wife is in the hands of her husband.

Do you want a glorious wife without spot or wrinkle, holy and pure? Then, love your wife as your own body! By so doing, you would have created a glorious wife. Love is the price you pay for a glorious home. It must be without hypocrisy, but rather sees good even while assessing a wrong situation.

I can boldly say that I don't know if my wife has done anything wrong, because even if she has, I know that it must have been in a bid to do the right. For instance, if the soup is too salty, I'm sure it must have been in a bid to put enough salt. I have never spoken about her in any negative way, neither have I ever sat down to set a trap for her and deal with her on any issue. I don't expect her to go wrong, so she doesn't.

The first thing I check in any case of family crisis that is brought to me is the love responsibility of the man. Is he actually in love with his wife or is he only in a sexual relationship? Man, if you want a very submissive wife, be a super loving husband. That is the quickest way to win your wife. Once a man loves his wife as Christ loves the Church, the devil cannot gain access to his home. Love is the summary of God's covenant obligation for the man.

Let us see some expressions of love:

Giving

Giving is the practical expression of love.

> ***For God so loved the world, that he gave his only begotten Son, that whosoever believeth in him should not perish, but have everlasting life.***
>
> John 3:16

One of the ways a husband should express his love for his wife is by giving. A husband should willingly and joyfully give gifts to his wife. How much (quantity) is given is not the issue. He should rather accept his responsibility, by joyfully giving his wife gifts. That is what counts.

Some men shy away from their responsibilities and don't give their wives home-keeping allowance, under the guise that their wives are working. This is not right!

It is not of God. The Scripture says:

> ***But if any provide not for his own, and especially for those of his own house, he hath denied the faith, and is worse than an infidel.***
>
> 1 Timothy 5:8

It is the man's responsibility to provide for the home. When a man stops looking after his household, his life becomes worse than that of an unbeliever's. No matter how much tithe and offering he gives, God says he has denied the faith and will suffer the same fate as an unbeliever.

The responsibility of providing for the home is the man's. It must be accepted joyfully, and executed excitedly. Be concerned about your wife and children's welfare. Some men leave home not concerned whether their family members have eaten or not. This is a violation of covenant obligations, and is very risky. No man has any right to wear new clothes, when his family is going about in rags. You should set aside some amount of money from whatever you earn, to cater for the personal needs of your wife and children.

> ***A good man leaveth an inheritance to his children's children: and the wealth of the sinner is laid up for the just.***
>
> Proverbs 13:22

In my family, for instance, I have a monthly allowance for everyone in my household. My children have their own personal accounts, I give my wife an allowance, which is apart from her income and house-keeping allowance. It is not how much that matters, but you accepting your responsibility and doing it joyfully. Where you are now is a good place, so start from there. Remember that life is in phases.

I have also taken steps to ensure that my children walk in the covenant of abundance. They all pay tithes and make kingdom investments from their monthly allowances and gifts they receive from people.

My wife has access to everything I own. In fact, all that is mine is hers. I love her with all my being, and am as committed to her as Christ is to the Church. Everything that concerns her welfare concerns me. Why? Because God expects me to nourish and cherish her as I would myself.

Prayer is not the way to marital success, neither is attending marriage seminars. The way to marriage success is by accepting responsibility for your home.

Communication

Love is also expressed in **communication.** I call it seasoned communication. Ephesians 5:26 says:

That he might sanctify and cleanse it with the washing of water by the word.

You are expected to cleanse your wife by the washing of water by the Word. That implies that every word of your mouth must be seasoned with salt, giving grace to the hearer (Colossians 4:6).

Love should be behind every observation you make. When you correct, rebuke or instruct your wife, it should be love-motivated. At no time should any unhealthy word proceed out of your mouth to her or your children. That way, you will present her to yourself a glorious bride, not having spot or wrinkle.

Likewise, ye husbands, dwell with them according to knowledge, giving honour unto the wife, as unto the weaker vessel, and as being heirs together of the grace of life; that your prayers be not hindered.

1 Peter 3:7

Husbands are under an obligation to honour their wives, as heirs together of the grace of life. This makes beating, humiliating or maltreating the woman a taboo. God expects you to deal with your wife according to knowledge. The knowledge of the truth will put you on top, such that even if your wife had a terrible character, by the application of the knowledge of the truth, you can change her.

It is the man's responsibility to be involved in his wife's affairs. I talked with a man some time ago. He told me what business his wife does. When I asked him his part in it, he said, "I don't have any position there." He was unknowingly digging a pit for himself by his nonchalant attitude.

Some husbands clearly see some things wrong in the home, and yet pretend that all is well. "God will take control", they say. But that is ridiculous! God has given man control of the home. Have you ever seen a driver taking his hands off the steering wheel and saying "God take control, I am tired"? If he does not handle the steering wheel, an accident is inevitable.

God has given you control as the head of the home; be a smart driver, otherwise that family is heading for an accident. For instance, if you notice that your wife is downcast, you should ask her what the matter is. You must not open up your home to malice or discord. You can prevail over them all by knowledge.

The Wife's Obligations

What God did at creation clearly reflects the position of the woman in the home. He took a rib from the side of the man to make the woman.

And the Lord God caused a deep sleep to fall upon

> ***Adam, and he slept: and he took one of his ribs, and closed up the flesh instead thereof;***
>
> Genesis 2:21

The fact that the bone was not extracted from Adam's head tells you that the man's position as head is incontestable. Also, the fact that the bone was not taken from Adam's feet proves that the wife is not to be trodden under foot or trampled upon as a slave.

It would be demonic for any Christian to question the leadership of Jesus over the Church. Similarly, any woman or women's organization that attempts to question the position of the man in the family should be regarded as being under a demonic influence. God expects that just as the Church is subject to Christ in everything, even so, women should be in subjection to their husbands in everything.

When a woman allows her husband to fulfill his covenant role of headship, she has automatically given him the room to play his messianic role over her. Sometime ago, my wife's health was under attack. I then went apart to inquire of the Lord what to do. As I searched the Scriptures, I discovered from Ephesians 5:23 that I am the saviour of my wife's body, the same way Christ is of the Church. I concluded, therefore, that my wife did not require her faith to be healed. I could exercise my God-given authority over her, as head of our home.

I returned home and learnt she was in the hospital. Without much ado, I had my bath, drove down to the hospital and ordered the doctor to remove all the medical gadgets that were on her and discharge her. Amidst protests from the doctor, I took my wife home.

The doctor came to our home later in the day to visit his patient, only to be told that she had gone to the hair dresser! The patient was no longer patient! That was the end of the bout with sickness.

If my wife was not reciprocating my love with submission, perhaps I would have become weary of loving her. But by submitting to me in everything, she gives me the co-operation I need to fulfill my "messianic" role in her life.

When my wife was in secular employment, she would always kneel down to present her salary to me at the end of every month. On one such occasion, when she presented her earnings, God told me to give it all as offering. Our first son was a baby then, and there was scarcity of baby formula. Even if there was money, the baby milk, like other essential commodities, was not available. So she would have been justified, especially as a mother, to question my decision. But all she said was, "Praise God."

However, after giving the money as offering, someone

drove to our home a few days later with an offering of 24 cartons of baby milk (without previous discussion)! If my wife had contested that decision, we would have missed that miracle, and perhaps gone through a period of hardship.

Often, the problem with many women is that they do not trust their husbands to make the right decisions. They keep struggling to make their points, so there is constant strife in the home. I wish women will strive for **proofs,** and not **points**!

If the man will love perfectly and the woman submits perfectly, then they will have a perfect home. Look at something interesting in Ephesians 5:33:

> ***Nevertheless let every one of you in particular so love his wife even as himself; and the wife see that she reverence her husband.***

The key word here is reverence. Once a woman lays hold on that key, she has succeeded in unlocking her husband's heart. You reverence your husband when his word counts in your ears and heart, and his instructions matter to you.

My wife has bought some clothes that I stopped her from wearing. Because my instructions matter to her, she never wore them. Success in marriage doesn't answer to fasting and prayer, but to a correct positioning in the covenant.

Even if a woman has an unbelieving husband, if her submission to him is absolute, she will wake up one day to see the man ready and eager to follow her to church. I saw from 1 Peter 3:1 that a woman does not need words to win her unsaved husband to Christ. Her actions can perform the miracle. Perhaps that is why Satan always moves her to talk uncontrollably, even though she wasn't created a talkative. Satan only wants to hinder her from making an impact in her husband's life.

Note that the submission I am talking about is not slavery, but submission in love.

> ***That they may teach the young women to be sober, to love their husbands, to love their children,***
>
> ***To be discreet, chaste, keepers at home, good, obedient to their own husbands, that the word of God be not blasphemed.***
>
> Titus 2:4-5

Submission has to be done in love, not out of fear or threats. When it is rooted in love, it is perfect and brings God's presence down in the home.

Also, note that if a woman doesn't submit to her husband, she would submit to someone else. The same is true for the man. If he doesn't love his wife, he would love someone else. It is, therefore, important that both husbands and wives fulfill their covenant obligations to one another. The end product will be success in family life.

MUTUAL OBLIGATIONS

> ***Let the husband render unto the wife due benevolence: and likewise also the wife unto the husband.***
>
> ***The wife hath not power of her own body, but the husband: and likewise also the husband hath not power of his own body, but the wife.***
>
> ***Defraud ye not one the other, except it be with consent for a time, that ye may give yourselves to fasting and prayer; and come together again, that Satan tempt you not for your incontinency.***
>
> 1 Corinthians 7:3-5

Romance greatly facilitates success in marriage. Unfortunately, however, this is where many Christians run into problems. When a home lacks romance, it starts suffering disintegration, as romance is one of the vital reasons for setting up the home. Many marriage teachers may not agree with this, but this is the Bible, and I absolutely agree with the Bible.

> ***...It is good for a man not to touch a woman.***
>
> ***Nevertheless, to avoid fornication, let every man have***

> ***his own wife, and let every woman have her own husband.***
>
> 1 Corinthians 7:1-2

One of the reasons for marriage is *"to avoid fornication."* Romance is God's tool for preserving marriage.

> ***But if they cannot contain, let them marry: for it is better to marry than to burn.***
>
> 1 Corinthians 7:9

The Bible says, *"Nevertheless, to avoid fornication, let every man* ***have*** *his own wife, and let every woman have her own husband."* The word "have" doesn't only mean to marry; it also means let him enjoy his own wife.

Rendering *"due benevolence"* means to give him or her, the benefit of marriage, which is your body. A husband and wife are to offer their bodies to one another. If a woman does not give her body to her husband, another person will, and vice versa.

God put in man a sexual desire, which should only be satisfied in marriage. That way, the desire will not be destructive. A sexually inactive marriage is heading for destruction. It is not God, but the devil a woman is praying to when her husband needs her and she says she is praying. When a husband starts speaking in tongues at the time his wife needs him, he is courting trouble.

This is where, I believe, some Christians have opened the door to trouble in their homes. The man is not available for his wife, so she looks somewhere else. The wife is not available for the man, so he goes somewhere else, because the burning must be satisfied.

The Bible says you mustn't allow your abstinence go beyond a time. Nobody fasts for one year. Learn to analyze Scriptures. The Bible says you can keep away from each other only for the reason of prayer and fasting. How long should prayer and fasting last? Jesus, the Messiah of the world, only fasted for forty days. That means you are permitted only forty days license to separate and come together again, lest Satan tempts you.

A healthy romance between a husband and wife makes for a healthy home and relationship. Romance is a great facilitator of a successful marriage. When a home stops being romantic, it starts to suffer devastation. The moment you stop desiring your spouse, you are already falling apart from each other. Lester Sumrall wrote a book entitled, *60 Things God Said About Sex.* These are men who had and enjoyed Christian homes.

To tell your wife today, "I am waiting on the Lord", tomorrow, "I am waiting on the Lord", next week, "I am waiting on the Lord." When you finish waiting, you won't find anybody again. Most crises in homes develop out of sexual tension. Romance in marriage is one of the areas you must intelligibly manage, because it reinforces the marriage covenant.

What Satan does is to sometimes use seemingly legitimate reasons, such as job opportunities, to separate couples. Whatever moves a man from his wife is Satan's way of luring them into adultery. He wants to draw them out of their Garden of Eden to the wilderness, so they will become wanderers.

Many homes have been ruined because the man is working in America or England and leaves his wife back in Nigeria. This is an open invitation to Satan. Matthew 19:6 says:

> ***Wherefore they are no more twain, but one flesh. What therefore God hath joined together, let not man put asunder.***

Money does not make a home; obedience is what does. In pursuit of money, many people have disregarded this important factor and teamed up with Satan to ruin their homes. The home is broken because the man has had to get an "assistant wife", since his wife is living far away.

The welfare of the wife is the primary responsibility of the man. God has put you in charge of that home to provide for it. You must accept your responsibility. That means you must not condone any form of separation, no matter how good a job your wife has or how fat her pay cheque is. The Lord help you, in Jesus' name.

Ten

Guaranteed Fruitfulness

– David

Unfruitfulness is a problem plaguing some marriages today. However, it is worth noting that marriage is designed for fruitfulness. With the same breath that God called forth light, and it came to be, He also said to man: ***Be fruitful, and multiply, and replenish the earth*** (Genesis 1:28).

That was not an admonition, but a commandment. God did not say, "You may be fruitful", but *"Be fruitful!"* God designed your marriage to be fruitful. Never mind whatever contrary report you may be holding in your hands now.

Fruitfulness should be natural to man, but when you are resisted by hell, you need an understanding of God's provision for your fruitfulness in marriage to combat the attack. The first thing to bear in mind is that God created you to be fruitful.

> ***And God said, Let us make man in our image, after our likeness: and let them have dominion over the fish of the sea, and over the fowl of the air, and over the cattle, and over all the earth, and over every creeping thing that creepeth upon the earth.***
>
> ***So God created man in his own image, in the image of God created he him; male and female created he them.***
>
> ***And God blessed them, and God said unto them, Be fruitful, and multiply, and replenish the earth, and subdue it: and have dominion over the fish of the sea, and over the fowl of the air, and over every living thing that moveth upon the earth.***
>
> Genesis 1:26-28

Everything God said when He was creating the world came to be. Therefore, it is impossible for what God has said concerning you and your home to fail. The counsel of the Lord stands for ever (Psalm 33:11), whatever He does abides till eternity (Ecclesiastes 3:14), nothing can be added to it or taken away from it.

So, since God has said to you, *"Be fruitful"*, blocked

fallopian tubes, low sperm count, or any such thing cannot stop that word from coming to pass in your life. Remember that He said, *"Let there be light"*, and there was light. So when He said to you, *"Be fruitful,* you must be fruitful.

Your fruitfulness is not dependent on your anatomy, nor does it have any bearing with the doctor's diagnosis or x-ray reports. Rather, it has everything to do with light from heaven. Remember that God's ways are not our ways, neither are His thoughts our thoughts (Isaiah 55:8-9).

All you need do to be fruitful in marriage is to believe that just as everything God said at creation is still in place, your fruitfulness is guaranteed. The Bible says:

> ***And blessed is she that believed: for there shall be a performance of those things which were told her from the Lord.***
>
> Luke 1:45

Therefore, it doesn't matter whether you are ovulating or not, or whether your sperm count is low. When you believe what God has said, there is a performance of those things which the mouth of the Lord has spoken.

The environment I grew up in was fraught with wickedness. I had lost a few of my relations to wicked machinations of the enemy. To worsen matters, before I got married, Satan had sworn to me that I would never have children. So, I needed to be sure I had encountered light from heaven concerning my fruitfulness.

That explains why, when I returned from a trip after I was married, and my wife told me that she had had a miscarriage, I reacted with, "It cannot happen! Can I have my food please?" I did not ask her how it happened or the case history; I simply reacted against it. Having failed to make me unfruitful, Satan wanted to destabilize me with a miscarriage. That was why I responded as I did, not because I didn't have any feelings for my wife.

To God's glory, the pregnancy was supernaturally sustained, and when the baby was born (exactly nine months after conception), he won an award for being the heaviest baby in the hospital! I named him *Makinde*. In my dialect, it means "another conqueror has come."

Trust In God

> ***They that trust in the Lord shall be as mount Zion which cannot be removed, but abideth for ever.***
>
> Psalm 125:1

I define trust as compound faith; that is, the kind of faith that makes you immovable, in spite of all odds. Trust is not conditional. It is not doing something as a prerequisite for God to do what He has promised. Trust brings you to a realm where you stand firm in God, irrespective of whether He does what He has promised or not. When you trust, it means you have discovered His provisions and are standing firmly on them.

Let me show you some of those provisions that will enable you to become rooted like Mount Zion, which cannot be moved, but abides forever.

> ***This is the book of the generations of Adam. In the day that God created man, in the likeness of God made he him;***
>
> ***Male and female created he them; and blessed them, and called their name Adam, in the day when they were created.***
>
> ***And Adam lived an hundred and thirty years, and begat a son in his own likeness, after his image; and called his name Seth:***
>
> ***And the days of Adam after he had begotten Seth were eight hundred years: AND HE BEGAT SONS AND DAUGHTERS:***
>
> Genesis 5:1-4

By the creation package before the curse came, you are also entitled to both sons and daughters. Therefore, be rest assured that nothing can hinder your fruitfulness.

> ***And ye shall serve the Lord your God, and he shall bless thy bread, and thy water; and I will take***

> ***sickness away from the midst of thee.***
>
> ***THERE SHALL NOTHING CAST THEIR YOUNG, NOR BE BARREN, IN THY LAND: the number of thy days I will fulfil.***
>
> Exodus 23:25-26

When God says: "*There shall nothing cast their young, nor be barren...*" He means there is no room for miscarriages or barrenness in your life. This is not subject to anyone's opinion. This Scripture liberated a woman who had been barren for 18 years. When I read it to her, she believed it, and that ended the reign of barrenness in her life. Simple as it may seem, it carries in it the power of God for performance.

> ***Thou shalt be blessed above all people: there shall not be male or female barren among you, or among your cattle.***
>
> Deuteronomy 7:14

This Scripture makes you understand that fruitfulness is not a promise, but a covenant. In Psalm 89:34, God assures us that He will not break His covenant, nor alter any word He has spoken. Your responsibility, therefore, is to believe this heavenly report, because it is your believing that brings it into reality. Therefore, fruitfulness in marriage is not a matter of luck, but **light** (understanding of its scriptural provisions).

These are the things I saw from God's Word that established my rest before I got married. God's perfect will for marriage is still fruitfulness, irrespective of the number of barren people you may know. His plan is superior to all negative human or biological excuses for barrenness in families. Here are a few testimonies of those who enforced God's will for their lives and took delivery of their covenant rights in God.

"In 1986, I noticed that I had not been having normal erection. This, I considered as nothing. I told no one about it, not even my parents. At this time, I was in my second year in the university. I was in this condition till after my NYSC, when my parents got to know about it, and from then on, we went to all sorts of sources, seeking for deliverance.

I had to travel from Kaduna to Imo in the east, in search of a cure. It was the mercy of God that saved me from being used for rituals in the process. In the church I was attending then, so many things were given to me to use, including black medicine. A lot of naira was spent on orthodox medicine too.

This was my situation until April 1995, when I first attended Living Faith Church in Kaduna. At this time, I was still on injections. I bought a cassette entitled, 'Provoking God's Blessings' by Bishop David Abioye.

After listening to the message, I went to the bank, withdrew 15,000 naira out of the 16,000 naira I had in my account, and brought it before God, for the painting of the Dominion Sanctuary that was being built then. I used the offering to provoke my healing.

One day in October, I came to the church premises with the remaining injections I had at home. I prayed to God and even had the opportunity of sitting on the Bishop's seat, declaring that since my pastor, Bishop David Abioye, was not impotent, I had nothing to do with impotence, and backed it up with Matthew 15:13, Isaiah 53:4-5 and Deuteronomy 7:14.

When I got up from the seat, I went out of the Frederick K. C. Price hall and broke the injections and trampled upon them, declaring that I would never use them again. To the glory of God, I regained my normal erection in the same month (October 1995)!

The Presiding Bishop, Bishop David Oyedepo, came from Lagos to declare the Faith Convention open. After his message entitled, 'Curse Warfare', he called out all those believing God for children. I went out with the other children of God and he prayed for us and pronounced God's blessings upon us.

To the glory of God, in the month of fruitfulness (February 1996), my wife announced to me that she was feeling like she had conceived, though she was still having her normal menstruation. On February 22, 1996, we went for a pregnancy test, but the test result was negative. I told my wife that they could not detect the pregnancy at that age.

After that, I knelt down before God and anointed the result, (thank God for the teaching Bishop Oyedepo gave us on the Law of nature and the Law of the Spirit). With this teaching in my heart, I declared the result as the result of nature, and that the Law of the Spirit says the pregnancy was there. We went for a second test, which was also negative.

All the while, my wife was having her menstruation and yet having all the signs of pregnancy. When we did the third pregnancy test, it was confirmed that my wife was 10 weeks pregnant! Since then, the pregnancy has been growing, waxing stronger and stronger." – **Olusola, S. A.**

"I *was here last year for the last Feet-washing service of the year, trusting God for the fruit of the womb.*

Precisely three months before my wedding, I stopped menstruating. After my wedding, I went to see the doctor. The first doctor said, 'Madam, I am sorry you'll find it difficult in taking in.' The second one said, 'Sorry, without menstruating, ovulation cannot take place, and without ovulation, you cannot get pregnant.' He also said, 'Tell your husband to get between ten thousand to one hundred thousand naira (₦10,000 to ₦100,000 Nigerian currency)ready, and I will carry out different tests, to know exactly what is wrong with you.'

Initially, I began to run from one hospital to the other, seeing various gynaecologists. Later, I got hold of one of the Bishop's publications, 'You Shall Not Be Barren'. The first paragraph I read said, 'There is no biological reason that is strong enough to hold married couples from getting pregnant, if they want to.' He further said, 'The Bible says, "Be fruitful and multiply"', so I said to myself, 'Menses or no menses, I am getting pregnant!'

At the last Feet-washing service in 1996, I came here and was sitting under the canopy. The Bishop said, 'Today, the devil will see you and cry'. I said, 'Amen'. He again said, 'Today, we are going to disgrace the devil and give God a serious dance.' I was really prepared. He further said, 'Matthew (song leader), come and lead us in worshipping God in the Ijesha dialect.' The talking drum was playing full swing, and I began to dance.

When it was my turn to wash my feet, I dipped my feet inside the water and said, 'Enough of barrenness, enough of unfruitfulness. Today, menses or no menses, I am getting my baby. I am coming here with my baby for the last Feet-washing service in 1997.' After that, I began to dance as if I was out in a competition.

My husband wasn't at the service, so when I got home, I told him, 'Look, our baby is ready' and he said, 'Okay'. In January, I went to the hospital to see my doctor. I told him, 'Look, I am pregnant.' He said, 'Okay, let's carry out the most accurate test, which is the blood pregnancy test.' But the result was negative. I went home and told my husband, and he said the doctor didn't see well.

I went back to the hospital in February and told my doctor, 'Check me, I am pregnant.' He said, 'Madam, I don't mean to frighten you, but I don't think you can be pregnant. I am sure it is because of your menstrual cycle. It is either you have PID (Pelvic Inflammatory Disease), ectopic pregnancy or the ovarian cyst is still disturbing you'.

But I said, 'Doctor, I cannot have any of these diseases.' He said, 'Why are you so sure?' I said, 'There is nothing like that from Genesis to Revelation.' He said, 'Madam, go and do a scan again.'

By the time I got to the scan doctor's door, I began to shake. The doctor said, 'But woman, I have scanned you before.' I said in my heart, 'God, don't make me a case study in this hospital.' The man placed his scanning machine on me and said, 'Woman, you are pregnant', and I began to cry. I said, 'Doctor, how many months pregnant?' He replied, '11 weeks and 4 days'. Today, I have my baby in my hand — a bouncing baby boy!" – **Olowosuko, A. (Mrs.)**

"At the Anointing Service of the September 1995 Breakthrough Seminar, the Bishop, while preaching shared a testimony of a man, who in his office had not been sent abroad on course, unlike his other colleagues. He said this man one day, moved by the Holy Ghost, brought his international passport to the church and rubbed it on the altar. That same day, on getting to the office, his boss asked him if he had an international passport, to which he answered in the affirmative, and he was sent abroad on course.

When the Bishop finished saying this, I said, 'God, I thank You, because I have contacted a miracle.' I was moved by the mystery of faith that moved the man to rub his passport on the pulpit, and I decided within me that if God could do it for the man, then I would come and do likewise, for the Lord to step into my own situation as well.

So, the following day (Sunday), I came here with two things — my mother's passport and my tummy. I had been married for 12 years, but had no child yet. Like the man in the testimony, I went to the altar, and began to rub my tummy on it. I said, 'Lord, the way You did it for that man, do it for me.' Lo and behold, I took in! This is my baby, Mary Onyekachukwu Anuoluwapo Chude. She was delivered on June 22 1996!

I asked for a smooth labour and safe delivery, like the Hebrew women, and I got it!" – **Chude (Mrs.)**

Eleven

Nurturing Your Godly Seed

– Faith

> ***And did not God make [you and your wife] one [flesh]? Did not One make you and preserve your spirit alive? And why [did God make you two] one? Because He sought a godly offspring [from your union]. Therefore take heed to yourselves, and let no one deal treacherously and be faithless to the wife of his youth.***
>
> Malachi 2:15 (AMP)

One reason why God makes husband and wife one in spirit and flesh is because their union is supposed to produce godly seeds. Although it is true that God commanded man to multiply and replenish the earth, His cardinal reason for childbearing is to raise up godly seeds unto Himself. But for God to have godly seed, there must be godly parents, for like begets like.

> ***Train up a child in the way he should go: and when he is old, he will not depart from it.***
>
> Proverbs 22:6

There is a way each child should go, and parents have the responsibility of locating and training them in it. When they do, the children will not depart from that way when they are old.

Parents should bear it in mind that the children of today are the adults of tomorrow; they constitute the future generation. Someday in future, the young parents today would become grandparents, and would have handed over the baton to the next generation. I pray that it will be to a godly generation.

The many atrocities in our world today, are a direct result of improper child training. Drug addicts, armed robbers and fraudsters are all from families, as no one dropped from the sky. But because their foundation was faulty, they become the dregs of the society. In the light of this, Christian parents must ask themselves what legacy they are leaving behind for their children. Nothing can be compared with a sound upbringing.

A mistake parents often make is to assume that the church, society or school is responsible for the training of their children. Although these agencies have certain contributions to make towards child training, the bulk is with the home. This is because growing children spend a greater percentage of their time at home. Thus, the home plays a major role in the upbringing of children. This, therefore, calls for a re-ordering of our priorities.

To Mothers

> ***A wise son maketh a glad father: but a foolish son is the heaviness of his mother.***
>
> Proverbs 10:1

> ***The rod and reproof give wisdom: but a child left to himself bringeth his mother to shame.***
>
> Proverbs 29:15

These Scriptures are addressed directly to mothers. I believe that though child training is a joint responsibility of parents, mothers have a greater share of that responsibility. This is so because among other things, mothers have a lot of influence over their children. By God's design, a man is vested with the power of authority, while a woman is vested with the power of influence. All through scriptures, you find women who used this power of influence to order the course of their children's lives.

Sarah used her power of influence to ensure Abraham sent Hagar away, so that Isaac can covenantly inherit his place in destiny (Genesis 21:10-12). Rebecca used hers to give Jacob the covenant blessings from Isaac (Genesis 27:9-29). Deborah used hers to get Barak courageous enough to go to battle (Judges 4:8), Abigail saved her family from massacre (1 Samuel 25:23-25). Even Elizabeth ensured that John the Baptist was not misnamed out of his destiny (Luke 1:59-61), just to mention a few examples.

Child training is, therefore, a must for every mother who does not want to be brought to shame.

Femininity is a unique attribute women are endowed with, which is necessary for the correct training of children. Femininity makes us tender as women. There is no child that does not need the feminine touch to be well nurtured. That is why it is anathema to see women struggling to be like men, wanting to be masculine, rather than being tender as God has created them. Men are created to be masculine, whereas women are created to be feminine. Our children require our "womanliness" to be brought up well.

Can you imagine an all-male world? There will be no tenderness or colour in it. All the colour will be grey, black or blue. Women are the ones that add pink, yellow and green to life.

Of course the men have their part in child training, but the role of the women is very vital and unique. Children who are brought up by their fathers alone (due to whatever reasons) have a masculine outlook to life, even if they are girls. Mothers add a graceful touch to the lives of their children.

The feminine nature of a woman is expected to be used for the raising of godly children, not negatively.

The **womb** and **breasts** are two special attributes which link women to their children. Children are nurtured in their mother's wombs and fed from their breasts. This is an advantage and privilege of motherhood that fathers don't have. What wonder of womanhood!

Mothers, whose children have run away from home, are backslidden or are problematic, can use these special features as a point of contact in praying for them. Wherever that child may be, you can call his name, put your hand on your womb or breasts, make your declarations and establish them on God's infallible Word, and it works!

Time Investment

In a bid to make it in business or career, some parents neglect to spend time with their children. They are too busy making money. They leave their homes early in the morning and return late at night, particularly those in the cities. They keep busy trying to make ends meet financially, but unfortunately, they seldom do. I believe one of the reasons why the efforts of such parents sometimes yield poor results, is because they have neglected their primary responsibility of nurturing their children.

Some parents, in a bid to have more time for their business concerns and other personal things, send their children to boarding schools. This is not to say that boarding schools in themselves are wrong. But if the motive behind sending your children is to shift responsibility, then it is wrong, no matter the type of boarding school they go to. Such parents see children as burdens, rather than blessings from the Lord (Psalm 127:3).

The destinies of many children have been marred because they were left to house helps (or 'dishelps' as the case often is) to raise. The Church is being robbed of her future great men and women, because many godly parents are producing ungodly children. Our responsibility is to stop the intention of the devil over the lives of our children, by investing time in their proper upbringing.

So, mothers, please create time to order and shape the

lives of your children. Do not leave them at the mercy of circumstances and situations. Don't allow them to learn what you ought to teach them from friends and television. Some children are faced with challenges too big for them to handle without right counsel. If you are not there to give them the counsel required, they turn to their friends, who might give them wrong counsel.

The world we live in now forces young children to mature fast. It exposes them to information that were hitherto restricted to adults. Therefore, we must not toy with our children's destinies. They may be small today, but you hold in your hands a great destiny.

Realizing the awesomeness of this responsibility, I personally cried to God for His grace. I don't want to fail Him. I don't want to face Him on the Day of Judgment and have nothing noteworthy to present, when asked what I have done with the destinies committed into my hands.

To further buttress this point, let me share a sister's testimony with you.

This sister got home late from work one day and as her habit is, she woke up her four-year-old daughter, and began to find out how her day at school was that day. The daughter suddenly said, "Mummy, I hate my gate man." Shocked, this sister asked her why. She then said because the gate man threw her Aunty (class teacher)'s bag into the waste basket. The sister immediately took spiritual charge of the situation, rebuking the spirit of bitterness and hatred and forbidding it from gaining access into the tender heart of this little child.

The following morning, she had the matter investigated. It was discovered that while the child was waiting for her parents beside the gate house, the teacher wanted to take a quick dash across the road to get something and left her bag with the gate man. The gate man, in a bid to keep the bag safe, in the midst of the rowdiness of closing hours, decided to keep the bag in his waste paper basket for safe keeping. This was what the child saw that was misinterpreted.

Can you even imagine what would have become of that child, had the mother not taken time to talk with her that night? The root of bitterness would have been planted and become a tree before the mother even takes note of it. So many mothers miss out on some very important issues happening around their children because they never find the time.

Some Worthy Examples

Many parents in the past have successfully raised their children, some of whom grew up to become assets to

God in their generation. Here are a few examples:

Timothy

> ***When I call to remembrance the unfeigned faith that is in thee, which dwelt first in thy grandmother Lois, and thy mother Eunice; and I am persuaded that in thee also.***
>
> 2 Timothy 1:5

Timothy became one of the most respected Bishops in the New Testament. Behind his outstanding success is the influence of his mother and grandmother, Eunice and Lois.

Timothy was such a godly seed, that he was well reported of by the brethren. He had such a good testimony that Paul would have him as a companion (Acts 16:1-3). God is looking for more Timothys. In this sinful and adulterous generation, may you be able to raise godly seeds like Timothy, who will fulfill their destinies in God.

> ***And that from a child thou hast known the holy scriptures, which are able to make thee wise unto salvation through faith which is in Christ Jesus.***
>
> 2 Timothy 3:15

How could Timothy have been taught the Scriptures without the active involvement of his parents? How the Church needs more of the likes of Eunice and Lois today!

Jesus

The excellent results Jesus had in ministry is rooted in His excellent upbringing. Although not much is written about Joseph, the influence of both Joseph and Mary is discernible in Jesus' life and ministry. They were such responsible parents that Luke 2:51 says:

> ***And he went down with them, and came to Nazareth, and was subject unto them: but his mother kept all these sayings in her heart.***

The fact that Jesus was subject (obedient) unto His parents shows that they did a good job in training Him, else Jesus would have rebelled or objected to their ungodly training.

I believe that because both Mary and Joseph fulfilled their parental responsibilities, there was no vacuum created in the life of Jesus. When He needed to be in the carpenter's shop, He was there as the son of Joseph. He could well have said, "I am the Son of God, I won't go to the shed today." But He remained submissive to them. I don't think that was ordinary.

Mary, especially, played her part in His training. As a matter of fact, it was Mary, who as a result of her sensitivity, knew when it was time for Jesus to manifest His glory. She understood the stages of His life. When Mary approached Jesus and told Him of the need for wine, Jesus responded, *"Woman, what have I to do with thee? Mine hour is not yet come."* She did not get angry or feel embarrassed at His response. She neither rebuked nor nagged Him for His reply. Rather, she went to the servants and said to them, *"Whatsoever he saith unto you, do it."* What a mature and self-controlled woman!

That was perhaps why even with nails fastened in His hands and a crown of thorns on His head, in the midst of pains and agony, Jesus could still remember to hand Mary over to John (John 19:26-27). Even when everybody else had deserted Jesus, her feminine nature would not let her go.

Nothing happens by chance. If you sow good seeds by training your child well today, he will reciprocate later in life. May your children be able to remember you tomorrow and call you blessed!

Daniel

> ***But Daniel purposed in his heart that he would not defile himself with the portion of the king's meat, nor with the wine which he drank: therefore he requested of the prince of the eunuchs that he might***

not defile himself.

Daniel 1:8

Daniel, a captive son of one of the princes of Israel distinguished himself in the land of Babylon. Although living amidst gross corruption, he purposed in his heart not to defile himself, and his desire was granted.

I believe one of the secrets of his success was the good upbringing he received back at home. He knew the difference between righteousness and sin. Even in the land of captivity, he was a man of good character in a world of compromise. He didn't want to defile himself, so he boldly went to make his request known to the chief of the eunuchs.

He was able to do this because he had been taught the law of God by his parents. No wonder when he was grown up, he did not depart from it.

Joseph

There is none greater in this house than I; neither hath he kept back any thing from me but thee, because thou art his wife: how then can I do this great wickedness, and sin against God?

Genesis 39:9

Joseph was also a slave in a strange land. His boss's wife vexed him daily to lie with her, yet he would not, because the fear of the Lord had been planted in his heart from home.

Arise To Your Responsibility

Let me give you some keys for effective child training.

The Word of God

> ***Thy word is a lamp unto my feet, and a light unto my path.***
>
> Psalm 119:105

It is your responsibility to impart the light of God's Word into your children. Once light gains access into them, no matter where they find themselves on earth, it becomes impossible for darkness to overcome them. When the light shines in them, they will become masters of darkness.

> ***Wherewithal shall a young man cleanse his way? by taking heed thereto according to thy word.***
>
> Psalm 119:9

You must spend time in teaching your children the Word of God. If they are too small to read, you can read to their hearing. You can also use picture books, drama, etc. Let the Word dwell richly in them. Do whatever is within your power to sow the good seed of

God's Word in them. Invest in good Bibles, Christian literature, audio and video tapes. What you're doing is nurturing them in the way of the Lord. You are sowing a good seed that will bring in a tremendous harvest tomorrow.

Love and Control

Love and control are two essential ingredients for child training. Every child needs to be **loved**. But at the same time, and of equal importance, is the need for **control**. Both go hand in hand in producing godliness in children. Be generous with love. Express it in words of praise and actions. Let the child be assured of your love, that way, it will be easy to control him.

By control, I don't mean turning your child into a puppet. I mean being able to restrain him and put a check to certain excesses in his life, enforcing discipline. A child that you do not love, you will not be able to control; and a child that you do not control, you cannot claim to love.

Expect Your Wages

> ***And Pharaoh's daughter said unto her, Take this child away, and nurse it for me, and I will give thee thy wages. And the woman took the child, and nursed it.***
>
> Exodus 2:9

There is profit in child training. There are wages for you when you train your child well. This may come in various ways. It may be monetary or otherwise. One of such wages is joy.

> ***A wise son maketh a glad father: but a foolish man despiseth his mother.***
>
> Proverbs 15:20

When you train your child aright, every remembrance of him brings joy to your heart. The more you labour in bringing him up, the more reward you stand to receive. As you accept your responsibility and raise up godly seeds unto the Lord, you will have cause to rejoice in the future.

You Can Make It

> ***For this is the love of God, that we keep his commandments: and his commandments are not grievous.***
>
> 1 John 5:3

The task of child training often appears awesome, but the good news is that God will not ask you to do what is impossible. Ruth Bell Graham once said, "As a mother, my job is to take care of the possible and trust God with the impossible."

Many people have succeeded in raising godly children, so we can make it by relying on God's grace, and arising to our responsibilities. You can also make it, in Jesus' name!

Child Training

– David

> ***Train up a child in the way he should go: and when he is old, he will not depart from it.***
>
> Proverbs 22:6

God has given parents the responsibility of training their children in His way. One of the best training tools is example. Training by example can accomplish for you what years of instructions cannot. One proof carries more impact than a hundred points.

Demonstrating the virtues you want your children to imbibe is more powerful than caning or even teaching them. Your examples are what stick with them, not the volume of words you speak. After all your points are forgotten, your examples will remain.

I learnt virtually every valuable thing I know today from my grandmother, who I grew up with. For example, I saw her work very hard, so I came to appreciate the virtues of hard work. She was quite comfortable, so putting two and two together, I figured that it must be hard work that resulted in her financial comfort.

One day she told me, "Don't look for relations; look for work, and relations will look for you!" She was not owing anyone when she died; rather, she had a long list of those owing her! Even at that, she kept telling us that nobody likes to borrow, so that if her debtors are unable to pay, we should not harass them.

I also imbibed the principle of tithing from her. Every Sunday morning, I always saw her take her tithe to church. When I asked her why, she said, "This is God's part of your labour, so that God can bless what remains." Although she did not know how to read, she taught me the principle of tithing.

My grandmother taught me how to trust people by trusting me. She gave me the key to her drawer where her money was kept, and put me in charge of her money. She would say in my hearing, "My son can never steal. He does not lie." So she showed me how to trust people, and it has paid off for me.

All these training have reflected in the running of the ministry God committed into my hands. Hard work has become a part of me. I don't need encouragement to pay tithe, and I am able to trust my workmen. When I travel, no matter for how long, I don't get worried about the ministry accounts or the like.

Some Christian parents today shout abusive words

at each other, commit all manner of atrocities, and yet teach the Word of God to their children. But as I said earlier, when all your points are forgotten, your examples will remain. Please leave a good example for your children. Remember that an ounce of example is worth a ton of preaching. You may think that they are too young to know what is happening, but they see the way you sit with your friends gossiping. It is a bad example.

Children should not be raised by shouting or caning, but by examples. Your responsibility is to leave footprints in the sands of time for them to follow. Sometime ago, my son saw me taking out some clothes from my wardrobe, preparing to give them out. "Do you want to give all these out again?", he asked. I said, "Yes. That's the way we got them in the first place by giving." Then he said, "Okay."

At another occasion, I needed to be in the office unusually early. My wife was not sure whether I took my bath before leaving, so she asked my first son if I had my bath before leaving. His reply was, "You know his bath is usually done in five minutes!" I don't remember telling him that, but he just knew!

Your children are watching the way you kick their mother around, and the way you insult their father. As a result, they say, "If this is marriage, I don't think it is really necessary for me." Think of it, certain things that happened to you in primary school are still fresh in your memory till now. Don't make the mistake of thinking, therefore, that your children are too small. They know what is happening.

Some women specialize in poisoning their children's minds against their father. But it is only a matter of time before they discover that Ephesians 6:2 says:

Honour thy father and mother...

In conclusion, you have a responsibility to raise your children principally by example, build up their destinies, and bring them forth as children of dignity.

Twelve

The Little Foxes

- Faith

> ***Take us the foxes, the little foxes, that spoil the vines: for our vines have tender grapes.***
>
> Song of Solomon 2:15

I had an opportunity of seeing a fox sometime ago. I was amazed at its size. It was really small, like a big cat. But as I looked at it, my mind went to the Scripture quoted above. I marvelled that something so small could actually destroy a vineyard that took years of labour to grow.

Foxes are usually identified with destruction in Scripture. In Judges 15:4, Samson caught three hundred foxes, and used them to burn and totally destroy the stocks, standing corn, vineyards and the olives of the Philistines.

There are some little foxes in marriage. They are little things that some may think are too insignificant to merit any attention. But it is amazing to discover that as little as they are, they have spoilt many marriages. Marriage can be likened to a vine having tender grapes. These foxes cause destruction of all sorts in marriages and families, if not checked. Let us examine some of them, so we can uproot them from our marriages and homes.

The Fox Of Bitterness

> ***Looking diligently lest any man fail of the grace of God; lest any root of bitterness springing up trouble you, and thereby many be defiled;***
>
> Hebrews 12:15

Bitterness starts from very little things. Perhaps your spouse or a family member has done something to hurt you, and you refuse to forgive him or her. Every remembrance of the incident brings pain to you. Watch it! That's a root of bitterness springing up gradually. If it is not dealt with immediately, it will ultimately trouble you.

The term "springing up" connotes a thing that starts small, and then suddenly shoots up. Once bitterness gains access into your heart and it is not immediately nipped, very soon, it will magnify itself and dominate you.

Another thing about bitterness is that it actually troubles and embitters individuals. You lose your rest to bitterness. If you're bitter against your spouse, when he or she is in the parlour you will want to be in the bedroom; there's usually no rest within you.

Also, bitterness makes you to fall short of the grace of God. That means when you harbour bitterness, you are actually frustrating the grace of God in your life. What are you without His grace? 1 Corinthians 15:10 says: ***But by the grace of God I am what I am...*** So, whereas you need His grace to succeed in your family, bitterness can frustrate that grace.

Bitterness also defiles. Not only does it trouble individuals, it goes beyond that to defile the person. It makes people filthy before God, as He sees you as an infidel and an outcast. In the Old Testament, outcasts were not permitted to dwell among other men (Isaiah 16:3). What a misery!

Simon had no part or lot in the Kingdom of God because his heart was not right in the sight of God. The root of his problem was defined in Acts 8:23 — ***...Thou art in the gall of bitterness, and in the bond of iniquity.***

Bitterness was the root of his problem, and he paid dearly for it. May you not lose your part in God's kingdom to bitterness.

Again, bitterness is a root that grows into the tree of unforgiveness. Wherever you see unforgiveness, know that bitterness is at its root.

The Price of Bitterness

There is a price for bitterness and unforgiveness. The incident in Matthew 18:23-35 is a good example. A man who was owing 10,000 talents begged his creditor to be patient with him till he was able to pay back the money owed, and his creditor forgave him the debt. But this same man saw a fellow servant who was owing him only 100 pence, and refused to forgive him, but threw the man into prison. As a result of his unforgiveness, he was classified as being wicked.

Unforgiveness is wickedness! An unforgiving wife, husband or child is a wicked person. Do you want to be identified with the wicked?

Secondly, his Lord was angry with him. So also does unforgiveness invite God's anger. Let go of unforgiveness, so God won't be angry with you.

The unforgiving servant was also delivered to the tormentors. Unforgiveness and bitterness torments.

Afflictions such as poverty, barrenness, sickness and the like in marriage are from the tormentors, as a result of unforgiveness. Unforgiveness opens the door to the tormentors of life.

The servant never enjoyed his master's forgiveness, in the same way that embittered people never enjoy forgiveness from God, because what you sow is what you reap (Genesis 8: 22). What a price!

Remedy

What must you do to overcome bitterness? Forgive! Forgive whosoever has offended you. Don't wait for the person to come and apologize to you, because he may not. Learn the secret of instant forgiveness. That is, forgive as soon as you are offended, whether the offender asks for it or not.

The Bible says: ***Let all bitterness...be put away from you, with all malice*** (Ephesians 4:31). So, forgive all family members that have offended you, so you can live a peaceful and burden-free life.

This is one of the secrets of success in marriage and family life. For wherever envy and strife are, there is confusion and every evil work (James 3:16). Many have lost their homes and marriages to bitterness; you don't have to join them. This principle of instant forgiveness has helped me a great deal. My husband and I practise it, and it has paid off for us. It pays to forgive!

The woman in the following testimony, made a choice to refuse offence and bitterness and even kept praying for her husband until not only did God save his soul, her home was also reunited blissfully after twenty six years.

26 Years Broken Marriage Restored!

"I got married 26 years ago. After just one year of marriage, my husband left me for another woman.

In fact, he gave me a letter of divorce however, but I did not accept it. I tried all possible ways to dissuade him from his plans, but failed

It was not easy at all. Everything around me kept saying it was over, but my spirit believed that reconciliation was on the way.

Since I saw it, I kept my focus without wavering. I never stopped praying and thanking God for the restoration that I was seeing.

In February 2004, he called me and told me that if I should die before him, he would bury me as his wife. Also, he said in case he should die first, I should know that he died as my husband; but that coming together was not going to be possible again.

He admitted making some mistakes, emphasizing that he was prepared to live with them for the rest of his life.

His statements gave me a prayer point. I told God to please help remove the sense of guilt from him, as I have forgiven him. This was exactly a year, after he spoke those terrible words to me.

On getting home, the first thing he told me was that he has given his life to Christ. He said that he wanted reconciliation, as he now knows that the divorce is not God's will.

We prayed together, and the 26 years of separation was terminated. Now our home is blissful and the favour of God is thick around us! Praise be to His name forever!"
- Mrs. Manya M.

The Fox Of Pride

Pride goeth before destruction, and an haughty spirit before a fall.

Proverbs 16:18

Pride and destruction are twins. Wherever you see pride, know that its companion, destruction, is also close by. The devastating effect of pride can be seen in the life of Lucifer. He was the son of the morning, the anointed cherub that covereth. He was beautiful, made of all manner of precious stones, a commander of a third of God's angels, but the moment God spotted pride in him, He cast him down to hell (Isaiah 14:12-15).

Pride abases. It leads to a fall. It brings destruction. Anytime you give room to pride, you are indirectly inviting destruction. It sets God against a man, because God resists a man of pride and if God resists a man, who can help him?

> ***Likewise, ye younger, submit yourselves unto the elder. Yea, all of you be subject one to another, and be clothed with humility: for God resisteth the proud, and giveth grace to the humble.***
>
> 1 Peter 5:5

Pride is very devastating. It begins from the heart, and has destroyed many homes. My husband often says, "If you're proud, you know it; you don't need a prophet to tell you." It is pride that makes a woman despise her husband, perhaps because she is better educated or paid.

In fact, some ladies are not married yet, not because no man is interested in marrying them, but because pride makes them see the men that come to ask them for marriage, as not being up to their standard. She looks at them arrogantly, and concludes that they cannot cater for her. She wants a man with a big car, a high-paying job, a house, etc. She is so full of herself and thinks she is too much for every man, and therefore looks down on them. But Zechariah 4:10 says:

> ***For who hath despised the day of small things? ...***

Pride will make such a lady a spinster for life. Walk in humility, and God will visit you.

It is pride that makes a man treat his wife as a slave, because he sees her as a nobody. He sees himself as the lord of all in his home, and the lion of the tribe of his home. So, every member of his family is scared of his presence.

Some parents are stumbling blocks to their children. They size up their daughter's suitors and conclude that she cannot marry him, perhaps because of his "low" social or academic status. Beware, because pride is a major hindrance to a glorious home.

Remedy

God has nothing to do with the proud and arrogant. The cheapest way to having a sweet home is to make yourself of no reputation. Take on a meek spirit, not minding what name people will call you. You have a lot to gain by being meek. God will not only guide you, He will also teach you His ways.

The Fox Of Wrong Company

He that walketh with wise men shall be wise: but a companion of fools shall be destroyed.

Proverbs 13:20

A man doesn't have to be foolish in himself to be destroyed. All he needs to do is walk with the foolish; soon, the folly of his friend rubs off on him and he is destroyed the same way a foolish man would. Walking with a foolish man is as bad as being foolish.

It is clear from the above Scripture that the company a man keeps can either make or destroy him. The company you keep either makes or mars you; it doesn't leave you the same. A wise man once said, "You will remain what you are today in five years time, except for the books you read and the company you keep."

The major cause of problems in some homes today is wrong association. Family members keep the wrong company, receiving counsel from people that stir up trouble perpetually in their homes.

I believe strongly in an adage that says, "Show me your friend, and I will show you who you are." It has a scriptural antecedent.

Can two walk together, except they be agreed?

Amos 3:3

Your friend is a reflection of you. A wrong association will affect you negatively. It will make you do things that you may ordinarily never do on your own. You must detach yourself from any child of Belial. Anyone that constantly provokes your spirit and gives you wrong counsel against your wife, husband or family well-being will destroy your home. Beware of partnering with even family members, who constantly tell you of only evil reports, about your husband or wife and even children.

> ***Be not deceived: evil communications corrupt good manners.***
>
> 1 Corinthians 15:33

Evil association corrupts good manners. The story of Amnon and his subtle friend Jonadab is a good example (2 Samuel 13). My husband believes that every wrong friend you keep is your enemy. Amnon paid for it with his life. After his death, Jonadab, the same "friend" who gave him wrong counsel was the one who announced his death.

Remedy

> ***Can two walk together, except they be agreed?***
>
> Amos 3:3

Agreement should be the basis for any association. Only agreeable people can relate profitably with one another.

Also, separate yourself from wrong friends. Who is your wife's friend? Who is your husband's friend? You have no business associating with anyone that brings tension to your home. Stop that association before it stops you! Receive grace to dissociate yourself from evil company, in Jesus' name. Remember Abraham had to separate from Lot before he could enter into the great things God had prepared for him (Genesis 13:7-17).

There is a need to be selective in your association. Select your friends in wisdom, as friendship is not by force. Even Jesus warns us to "beware of men" (Matthew 10:17).

The Fox Of Ingratitude

Ingratitude means unthankfulness. It is failing to acknowledge or appreciate acts of kindness either by God or man. The enemy uses it to distract man from seeing what God has done, to rather seeing what hasn't been done.

A man may be waiting on God for a life partner, but he is doing so with murmuring and complaining. He feels he has done all he ought to have done, that he qualifies for a wife. He feels that his mates are not only married, but already have children. Rather than see what God has done, he is wondering what his offence against God is. This is ingratitude to God.

You may not yet be married, but think about this: some who are the same age with you are insane, others are crippled. Instead of dwelling further on your plight, rise up in thanksgiving and praises unto God, for the great things he has done for you so far. Turn the reason for ingratitude into the object of thanksgiving. As you do so, you will encounter the God who is glorious in holiness and fearful in praises.

Another type of ingratitude is that towards your partner. Many husbands and wives do not appreciate the little kind acts of their partners. They never say, "Thank you." Though made up of just two words, saying "Thank You" can bring a lot of joy and peace to the home.

Some husbands have stopped providing for the home because their wives never appreciate their efforts. No matter how much they spend, it is never enough. At the other end are some husbands who find it difficult to appreciate their wives' inputs at home. No matter how much effort she puts into the smooth running of the home, he comes in from work and begins to find fault with all she has done, shouting and yelling at everybody. Very soon the woman will become weary, as she feels she can never please him. Learn to say "Thank you" for every little act of kindness, and see how exciting your marriage will become.

It is also necessary to appreciate the various inputs of those who live with you and lend a helping hand around the house. Even if you come home to discover that your house-help has done something wrong, don't start yelling at her and calling her names. You can start by acknowledging the things she has done right, and then call her attention to the things not well done. When she does something well, learn to say, "Thank you". Never forget that good words are worth much more and cost little.

You should also learn to say "Thank you" to your children when they do thank-worthy things. Remember, gratitude is what determines altitude.

The Fox Of Murmuring

> ***And when the people complained, it displeased the Lord : and the Lord heard it; and his anger was kindled; and the fire of the Lord burnt among them, and consumed them that were in the uttermost parts of the camp.***
>
> Numbers 11:1

> ***Neither murmur ye, as some of them also murmured,***

and were destroyed of the destroyer.

1 Corinthians 10:10

Complaining and murmuring always result in unrest in the home. If they brought fire to the camp of Israel, they will bring the same to any home.

Murmuring stops the help of God from reaching a man. Rather, it unleashes the destroyer. My husband often says, "Every complaint complicates issues for you." Don't complicate matters for yourself.

You have what it takes to take off the little foxes that spoil the vine. So, rise up to your responsibilities, and you will enjoy liberty.

- David

The Fox Of Ignorance

His mother saith unto the servants, Whatsoever he saith unto you, do it.

Jesus saith unto them, Fill the waterpots with water. And they filled them up to the brim.

John 2:5,7

When the family in Cana of Galilee was about to experience shame and reproach, Mary gave them the remedy — *"Whatsoever he tells you to do, do it."* That is still the secret of family triumph today.

Notice that Jesus instructed them to fill the water pots. That means, whatever the Word of God demands of you, do it to the full, without any reservations. Until they filled the pots up to the brim, the miracle did not take place. Ephesians 5:26 likens the Word of God to water. Therefore, when Jesus told them to fill up the water pots with water, it could be likened to filling them up with the Word.

Remedy

When you are filled with the Word concerning your home, it cannot run short of miracles. There is what to do to keep enjoying miracles in the home — keep doing whatever He tells you to do. Not just doing it, but doing it fully, that is, going to the extremes in your obedience.

For instance, until a woman is prepared to submit to her husband in all and with reverence, she will never experience lasting joy in her home. The Word of God has no respect for civilization, neither does it take cognisance of education, culture or anything else. It is forever settled in heaven. It has been signed and sealed. To be too smart for the Word is to opt for a life of misery. But you can have miracles of harmony, peace, joy, etc, if you do whatever He tells you to do.

God has not changed, and He will not compromise His standard. If you don't want to experience shame in your family, do what He tells you to do. For instance, Jesus' instruction to the servants in Cana was inconvenient. He instructed them to fill the water pots with water. They probably must have been ridiculed by men when they were doing so. They could have been laughed at, mocked and scoffed at, but as they carried out His instructions, they got their desired miracle.

When God's Word is not given its place of priority in the family, there's bound to be problems. When a man disregards God's Word, a time comes when he cries out for God's intervention, God will simply fold His arms, unperturbed (Proverbs 1:28-30).

A Christian home founded on the Word of God enjoys sweat-less triumph in the battles of life. Satan is rendered powerless when a couple stands firmly on the Word of God and operates by its principles. Marriage is very exciting if Biblical injunctions are adhered to, because the knowledge of the truth is what puts a man on top. Here are a few testimonies on the wise application of the Word of God:

"I used to worship in a place where the pastors believe that "misunderstanding brings about understanding." One day, the lady pastor asked me if I had ever had any serious quarrel with my wife (then my fiancé), and I said 'No'. She said we had not started, that until we

quarrelled and fought, we would not know if we truly loved each other.

We started having problems in our home after our marriage. But when I came here, I heard the Bishop say, 'I have not had the first argument with my wife.' I told my wife that if what the man of God was saying was the truth, then we've been in the wrong place, where we had been fed with the wrong food spiritually. So we decided to start worshipping here.

We told ourselves, 'What this man of God has seen that is making his marriage sweet, we also must discover it.' Then I was in WOFBI Full-Time programme. After each lecture, I would go back home and teach my wife the same thing. Today to the Glory of God, we don't have misunderstandings anymore!" — **Ibiang, A. I.**

"When I was ready for marriage, I noticed that some things were working against me. But I was not a serious Christian then. However, when I dedicated my life fully to Jesus Christ in 1992, it became obvious that I lacked wisdom and counsel and was emotionally immature. All the same, I got married, and the Lord has been merciful.

But on joining this church, from the different ministrations I received, my life and marriage became meaningful and received direction. Now my marriage is established, and I am free from all manner of oppressions of the wicked. My family has been increased remarkably, and I now apply myself to the wisdom of God that has been imparted to me here!" — **Opara, C. C. N.**

"Today marks three years since I started attending this church. What brought me here was my spiritual lack. I was born again five years before I came here and was attending a living church. But since I started worshipping here, God has given me the spirit of understanding, so that the Word of God and my faith has been on the increase. Most importantly, there has been captivity turnaround in my life, particularly in my marriage.

My marriage technically broke down on the wedding day, at the reception table! But I stayed on in it for almost a decade. It was a thorn in the flesh. Eventually, I had to leave. Right inside my matrimonial home, I got a SAN to prosecute the divorce.

I got born again after then, but the Word never came to me until I got to this church. There was a teaching on forgiveness one day, which made me realize that I had been living in self-righteousness all along. I forgive, but don't forget. I got this corrected in my mind and through the anointed book ***Marriage Covenant****, and anointed preachings and counselling of the men of God, my marriage was miraculously healed, and right now, I'm* *having a honeymoon."* **— Olaleye**

Let me reiterate that all you need to do to experience the miraculous in your home is what was done at Cana of Galilee — *"Fill the waterpots with water"* and do it without reservations.

There is nothing like luck or fortune in the kingdom. What obtains is knowledge. For instance, what is lucky about a man who gets saved? He simply heard the gospel and responded to it. He submitted to its instructions, and according to the Word, he's saved.

Similarly, when you hear the good news on anything, and respond to it, God confirms it. Let the man love his wife with all his heart and the woman submit to her husband in everything, and the cause of their misunderstandings will vanish. The truth will triumph.

I cannot remember ever going to God and saying, "Oh God, bless my family." He blesses us on His own, because we are doing what He says we should do. I recall the days when my wife was still in secular employment. When she received her salary, she would kneel down and hand it over to me. You may say that she is local, but that is your opinion. In fact, her handing over the money to me was a risk, because I could give it all to the next person who came in, if God commanded me to do so.

To you it may sound absurd and uncivilized, but I reckon that modernization is one of Satan's strategies for destroying Christian homes. All that my wife used to hand over to me as her income then were peanuts compared to what I give her now! I have bought several posh cars for her as surprise gifts. Now, by virtue of my placement in God, I can sign cheque leaves and leave them with her to fill in any amount she wants at anytime. I never return to ask her, "Why did you spend this or that?"

There is an adage in my dialect that says, "If you don't pour water in front, you won't tread on soft ground." It is time you followed fully the Word of God. There is no modern Christianity. You must stand in the way, according to Jeremiah 6:16, and see and ask for the old path, wherein is the good way where your fathers trod, and you shall find rest for your soul. The old path is still the good way.

Marriage is an institution established by God and must be sustained by His Word. If you fill the water pots with water, you will have sweeter wine everyday.

Thirteen

Wisdom For Establishment

- David

Through wisdom is an house builded; and by understanding it is established:

And by knowledge shall the chambers be filled with all precious and pleasant riches.

Proverbs 24:3-4

Wisdom is a builder of homes. It is in fact the master builder's trade secret. Paul in 1 Corinthians 3:10 says:

According to the grace of God which is given unto me, as a wise masterbuilder, I have laid the foundation, and another buildeth thereon. But let

every man take heed how he buildeth thereupon.

Once a home is founded on wisdom, the devil cannot pull it down. But even when the devil is a non-issue in a home, it can still be brought down by foolish hands.

> ***Every wise woman buildeth her house: but the foolish plucketh it down with her hands.***
>
> Proverbs 14:1

Therefore, wisdom is the builder of every home. It is more potent than prayer or fasting, because it is laying hold on and trading with the Word of God. A wise man is one who knows from God's Word which way to go and how to handle situations to produce the desired results.

When you are guided by Scriptures in every aspect of your life, you are walking in wisdom. This frustrates the devil, because he knows that your home is, by wisdom, founded upon a rock that no wind or storm can uproot. Jesus said:

> ***Therefore whosoever heareth these sayings of mine, and doeth them, I will liken him unto a wise man, which built his house upon a rock:***
>
> ***And the rain descended, and the floods came, and the winds blew, and beat upon that house; and it fell not: for it was founded upon a rock.***

> ***And every one that heareth these sayings of mine, and doeth them not, shall be likened unto a foolish man, which built his house upon the sand:***
>
> ***And the rain descended, and the floods came, and the winds blew, and beat upon that house; and it fell: and great was the fall of it.***
>
> Matthew 7:24-27

Wisdom is the secret for building a successful home, and it comes through three main avenues:

Instructions

> ***The tongue of the wise useth knowledge aright: but the mouth of fools poureth out foolishness.***
>
> Proverbs 15:2

Wisdom is the right use of knowledge, or the correct application of knowledge. In other words, knowledge is the raw material processed and developed into a finished product called wisdom. It, therefore, means that if you don't have the facts of a matter, you cannot arrive at wisdom. What wisdom does is to correctly apply the facts acquired in order to get your desired results.

To get at the best in anything, you need facts. Fact, is the father of success. Every success is fathered by **facts**. These facts are nothing other than the knowledge of God's Word.

Wise men lay up knowledge: but the mouth of the foolish is near destruction.

Proverbs 10:14

How much knowledge you lay up is what determines how much wisdom you can operate in. This shows the futility of seeking after wisdom without a hunger for knowledge. Some people believe that you can get wisdom through prayer, but I believe that prayer connects you to only a part of the wisdom.

The wisdom that comes through prayer is essentially inspirational, whereas the wisdom acquired from the Word (fact/knowledge) is dependable. Some are always on their knees, crying for wisdom. But a deliberate, determined and desperate search in the Word will link you up with greater wisdom and set you on the path of excellence, even in your homes. Notable wise men have a reputation for being men of knowledge too.

The heart of the prudent getteth knowledge; and the ear of the wise seeketh knowledge.

Proverbs 18:15

Wisdom is the trade secret of every master builder, and it hinges primarily on knowledge. That is why I Peter 3:7 instruct thus:

Likewise, ye husbands, dwell with them according to knowledge, giving honour unto the wife, as unto

the weaker vessel, and as being heirs together of the grace of life; that your prayers be not hindered.

Husbands should dwell with their wives according to knowledge. Knowledge is it, so get it (Proverbs 4:7).

Meditation

Having collected instructions from the Word of God, meditation is the next process to embark upon. Meditation is the process of reasoning, pondering or thinking through.

Whereas instructions from the Word can be likened to raw materials, meditation is the refining process. The life in the Word acquired can only be obtained and applied through the process of meditation. But unfortunately, it is at this point that many Christians fall short.

Meditation is an activity of the mind; it is a mental exercise aimed at achieving something definite. At salvation, your mind is not suspended, but upgraded to reason at a supernatural frequency. You undergo, as it were, a mind transplant, in which your natural mind becomes the mind of Christ (1 Corinthians 2:16). By the upgrading of your mental faculty, you are thus enabled to reason with God. He tells you freely: ***...Let us plead together: declare thou, that thou mayest be justified*** (Isaiah 43:26).

God wants you to be a deep thinker. He expects you to become a supernatural analyst, able to look at issues and rightly divide them. If there is something out of place in your family, you should be able to sit down and find out a solution from the pages of Scripture.

For example, if your husband slapped you yesterday, what you should do is to sit down and reason things out. Ask yourself, "What did I do to warrant a slap? What are the things that irritate him and lead to these regular slaps?" If you can reason your way through that, and avoid doing those things, you will be through. This is, however, not to justify husbands who slap their wives. No matter the provocation, there's a better way to handle it than with a slap.

The prodigal son reasoned his way out of shame back to glory. Nobody builds a tower without first sitting down and counting the cost (Luke 14:28). That's wisdom. I think ten times more than I pray, because when I am thinking, I am working together with God for definite results. I ask Him, "What must I do, Lord?" He shows me the way, and I do it.

When people talk about marital problems, I have no contributions to make along that line, so I wonder if we are living in the same world! But recognize that a hitch-free marriage is not a gift from God; it is a function of

His grace that is acquired through knowledge (2 Peter 1:2). I have never prayed for success in my home. All I do is locate what to do to succeed in it and keep doing them. As long as I do them, God is committed to my success.

There is good in the Word, but it is kept for those who will care to reason it out. There is also good in your marriage, but it is available only if you bother to reason. Knowing what to do is what makes family life colourful. There is no problem you are faced with in the home that has no solution with God. But those solutions come as you reason your way through, by meditation.

Planning

> ***Any enterprise is built by wise planning, becomes strong through common sense, and profits wonderfully by keeping abreast of the facts.***
>
> Proverbs 24:3-4 (TLB)

Family life is a covenant enterprise that is built through wise planning, becomes strong through common sense and profits wonderfully by keeping abreast with the facts.

For example, a man who has just started a family, has one child, and earns four thousand naira (₦4,000 Nigerian currency) must know what God expects him to do with his finances. The Holy Ghost won't plan for him. He must ask himself, "What is my tithe?" Four hundred naira (₦400). He is left with three thousand, six hundred naira (₦3,600), which he must wisely plan how to spend. Out of this, he should remove a certain amount for housekeeping, and if he is committed to the Kingdom, he should also set his offerings aside, and whatever is left he marks as miscellaneous. This is wisdom.

I remember that even when we were earning four hundred and forty naira (₦440 Nigerian currency) monthly i.e.(three hundred naira "₦300" for me, and one hundred and forty naira "₦140" for my wife), we never ran out of food to eat at home. I have always lived well, because I am a planner. My wife is also a very successful planner.

To run a successful home, you need to use your covenant sense and available facts to determine your budget. It is foolishness, to buy a new suit worth five thousand naira (₦5,000), when you know that your income is only four thousand naira (₦4,000). How do you intend to pay for the suit? Wearing clothes on hire purchase simply makes things more difficult for you.

If all you can afford to give in church per service is two naira (₦2) from your four thousand naira (₦4,000) monthly income, give it cheerfully. God does not put weights on anyone. Don't say that you are suffering because you're sowing into God's Kingdom. Serving God makes men to shine when they are walking in wisdom.

Zeal without knowledge is foolishness. So, be a wise planner. God knows your size per time, so give willingly and according to what you have, and very soon it will increase. One thing to remember is that every small thing becomes big through quality planning.

Some families are under strain because they put their children in schools that are beyond their income. There is no point praying and fasting to pay school fees every term; there is no wisdom in that. There is equally no wisdom in renting a house far beyond your income. To live comfortably, you need to be a smart planner. Planning is not a gift, but a task! It makes living colourful.

Wisdom is the principal thing; and with all your getting, get understanding. It will show you what next to do in your home to make it a place of beauty. Whatever is missing in your home, wisdom will help you locate it and put it in place.

So, receive a fresh impartation of wisdom right now, in Jesus' name! Amen.

Postscript

The Seven Concepts Of Marriage

- David

I have said so much about the seven concepts of marriage God gave me before I got married. I wanted to know God's purpose for instituting marriage, because the marriages I saw around me were not encouraging.

As I set myself in a search, studying and meditating on the Word of God, I located what I now call the *Seven Concepts Of Marriage.*

I went into marriage armed with these concepts, and my marriage has been a testimony. Marriage is not a necessary evil after all; it is a necessary good. Here are the concepts:

1 Marriage Is Good

And the Lord God said, It is not good that the man should be alone; I will make him an help meet for him.

Genesis 2:18

Marriage was instituted for the good of man. God didn't create it to trap any man's destiny. Marriage is designed to make life great, so when life is not great in marriage, it's a disappointment to the Creator. Marriage is nothing to be scared of, as it was designed to make life complete.

2 It Is For Better Living

How should one chase a thousand, and two put ten thousand to flight?...

Deuteronomy 32:30

Two are better than one; because they have a good reward for their labour.

For if they fall, the one will lift up his fellow: but woe to him that is alone when he falleth; for he hath not another to help him up.

Again, if two lie together, then they have heat: but how can one be warm alone?

And if one prevail against him, two shall withstand

him; and a threefold cord is not quickly broken.

Ecclesiastes 4:9-12

Marriage is for better living, as two are better than one! Something used to scare me in the marriage vows I heard people take in those days. They say such things as, "I, so and so, get into wedlock with you for better, for worse, in sickness and in health, in failure and in success..."

But what really is God's concept for marriage? Two are better than one! One shall chase a thousand, and two shall put ten thousand to flight. What did Jesus say about it also? He says:

Again I say unto you, That if two of you shall agree on earth as touching any thing that they shall ask, it shall be done for them of my Father which is in heaven.

Matthew 18:19

The greatest agreement under heaven is in marriage. It is the only relationship that gives room for unity in body, soul and spirit. Your spouse is the only one you can be committed to in the body.

3 It Is Designed For Fruitfulness

One of the major plagues in marriage is the plague of

unfruitfulness. But the manufacturer states very clearly that it is designed for fruitfulness.

The same Word that called light from wherever it came from is the same that called man fruitful.

> ***And God blessed them, AND GOD SAID UNTO THEM, BE FRUITFUL, AND MULTIPLY, AND REPLENISH THE EARTH, and subdue it: and have dominion over the fish of the sea, and over the fowl of the air, and over every living thing that moveth upon the earth.***
>
> Genesis 1:28

It is an order! If God said, *"Be fruitful"*, fallopian tube can't block it. If God said, *"Be fruitful"*, low sperm count can't stop that command. No sperm count was needed for Mary to be pregnant. Your being fruitful has no bearing with the chemistry of your body or the discoveries of the doctors. It has nothing to do with X-rays either.

This gave me rest, because quite a number of people around me then were agonising for children. As a result, I said, "If that's what marriage is all about, then I don't need it." But God said, "No, that's not My plan for creating marriage."

Please, know that nothing can stop you from being fruitful if you're married. His purpose is that you are fruitful, and no devil can stop that. You are entitled to both *"sons and daughters"* (Genesis 5:1-4).

Fruitfulness is not a matter of luck; it is in the creation package. You are entitled to both sons and daughters, so you can speak with the enemy at the gate. So, I say to you, that the enemy has said, cannot have a child, "Be fruitful, multiply, replenish the earth. Beget sons and daughters, in Jesus' name!"

4 The Law Of Departure

> ***...For this cause shall a man leave father and mother, and shall cleave to his wife: and they twain shall be one flesh?***
>
> ***Wherefore they are no more twain, but one flesh. What therefore God hath joined together, let not man put asunder.***
>
> Matthew 19:5-6

Anti-covenant interference from parents, relations and friends, is the source of some troubles in the home. God told me that the law of departure must be in place for one to be able to enjoy success in marriage. When that law is broken, you have opened the door to all manner of negative events.

Until you depart, you cannot cleave and until you cleave, you cannot know peace.

5 The Covenant Obligation Of The Husband

What does the manufacturer of the marriage institution expect from the husband?

> ***Husbands, love your wives, even as Christ also loved the church, and gave himself for it;***
>
> Ephesians 5:25

The making of any wife is in the hand of her husband. Do you want a wife without spots, wrinkle, or any such thing? Then love her! Men are to love their wives as their own bodies.

Until the love responsibility is accepted, there will be nothing called success in marriage. Knowing and accepting this responsibility made me to believe that if I were married to even the devil, he would be converted. Love will break the back of any devil trying to harass your family life.

6 The Covenant Obligation Of The Wife

> ***Wives, submit yourselves unto your own husbands, as unto the Lord.***
>
> ***For the husband is the head of the wife, even as Christ***

is the head of the church: and he is the saviour of the body.

Ephesians 5:22-23

The husband is not the side, he's the head. His headship cannot be contested. So when you allow your husband to be the head of the home through submission, he can then play the messianic role. He's the head, not your colleague.

Please note that the submission I'm talking about is not in slavery, but in love; not in fear, but in love. When submission is done in love, it is seen as perfect, and God will always show Himself.

7 Mutual Obligations

Romance

God's idea of procreation establishes the coming together of husband and wife (1 Corinthians 7:1-5). Many homes are broken today because of a lack of understanding of this concept. The moment a home becomes deficient in marital affairs or romance, it is beginning to break.

Sexual relationship is God's approved channel for procreation. Everything done against it by either the husband or the wife is targeted at the ruin of the home.

Providing For The Home

Let every man know that looking after your family is your primary responsibility. You are the one God put in charge of the home.

> ***But if any provide not for his own, and specially for those of his own house, he hath denied the faith, and is worse than an infidel.***
>
> 1 Timothy 5:8

Child Training

Also, we have a responsibility to train our children. Example is the best training tool. One proof carries much more impact than one hundred points, because when all your points are forgotten, your examples will remain. Please, show them good examples to follow.

Also, you don't raise children by caning them; you raise them by showing them good examples.

These seven concepts of marriage have been of immense blessing to me, and I believe they will be to you also. You shall enjoy success in marriage!

ABOUT THE *Author*

Dr. David Oyedepo is the President and Founder of Living Faith Church Worldwide a.k.a. Winners' Chapel International, with a network of churches across all cities, towns and most villages of Nigeria and over 60 other nations that spread across five major continents of the world. His faith-based teachings have literally transformed millions of lives.

To date, he has published over 60 highly impactful titles covering a range of issues, with over seven million copies in circulation.

He is the Senior Pastor of the 50,000 - seat church sanctuary - Faith Tabernacle, Canaan Land, Ota, a suburb of Lagos, Nigeria reputed to be the largest church auditorium in the world, where presently four services run every Sunday morning.

As an educationist, his mission is currently leading a revolution in education in Nigeria, with the establishment of educational institutions at all levels - primary, secondary and tertiary including the renowned Covenant University and the newly established Landmark University, where he serves as Chancellor. His educational movement is fast spreading to other African nations.

He is married to Faith and they are blessed with sons and daughters.

Books By Dr. David Oyedepo

- The Unlimited Power Of Faith
- In Pursuit Of Vision
- Pillars Of Destiny
- Signs & Wonders Today
- Exploits In Ministry
- Winning The War Against Poverty
- Walking In Dominion
- Possessing Your Possession
- The Wisdom That Works
- Exploits Of Faith
- Anointing For Exploits
- Understanding The Power Of Praise
- Walking In Newness Of Life
- Maximise Destiny
- Commanding The Supernatural
- Winning Invisible Battles
- Success Systems
- Understanding Financial Prosperity
- Success Strategies
- Understanding Your Covenant Right
- Miracle Meal
- Exploring the Riches of Redemption
- Anointing For Breakthrough
- Excellency Of Wisdom
- Breaking Financial Hardship
- The Release Of Power
- Walking In The Miraculous
- Satan Get Lost!

- The Winning Wisdom
- Walking In Wisdom
- The Healing Balm
- Manifestations Of The Spirit
- Breaking The Curses Of Life
- Overcoming Forces Of Wickedness
- You Shall Not Be Barren!
- Exploring The Secrets Of Success
- Winning Prayer
- Understanding The Anointing
- Fulfilling Your Days
- Towards Mental Exploits
- Understanding Vision
- Understanding Divine Direction
- The Force Of Freedom
- Born To Win
- The Shower Of Blessing
- Riding On Prophetic Wings
- All You Need To Have All Your needs Met
- Operating In The Supernatural
- Ruling Your World
- The Blood Triumph
- Keys To Divine Health
- Winning Faith
- Conquering Controlling Powers
- Put Your Angels To Work
- Covenant Wealth
- Keys To Answered Prayer
- Miracle Seed
- The Hidden Covenant Of Blessing

The Author

Faith Abiola Oyedepo has through the leading of the Holy Spirit, brought hope, joy, peace and life into many families and homes in her generation.

For many years that she received the ministry for families and homes, she has in no little measure dedicated her entire life to showing people the perfect will of God concerning their family relationships and homes. Her regular and scintillating weekly newspaper and internet columns - Family Matters, Family Success and Family Life, among others - have helped in no small way in achieving this goal.

Also, she is reaching out to the less privileged, the needy and those in the valley of decision, through her Faith Abiola Oyedepo Foundation (FAOF).

She has a divine mandate to make her shoulders available and enrich the lives of singles and unmarried persons in a unique way.

Pastor Faith has written over 20 anointed and impactful books that have transformed many lives and given them a change of story, including her best-selling title: *Rescued From Destruction.*

An anointed preacher of the Gospel, Pastor Faith has been doggedly supportive of her husband [Dr. David O. Oyedepo, the Visionary/President Of Living Faith Church Worldwide Inc.] in the work of the ministry.
They are the parents of four grown children – David Jnr., Isaac, Love and Joys.

Books By Faith Oyedepo

- Building A Successful Family
- Making Marriage Work
- Success In Marriage
  (Co-authored with Dr. David Oyedepo)
- Marriage Covenant
- Raising Godly Children
- Rescued From Destruction
- Single With A Difference
- The Effective Minister's Wife
- The Spirit Of Faith
- A Living Witness (Expanded version)
- Nurturing The Incorruptible Seed (Expanded version)
- Service: The Master Key (Expanded version)
- The Dignity Of The Believer (Expanded version)
- Growing In Grace
- The Power Of The Communion Table
- Healing, Health And Wholeness
- Overcoming Anxiety
- Salvation: The Way Of Escape
- The Healing Scriptures
- The Healing Ministry Of Jesus Christ
- You Are Welcome To God's Family
- Understanding Motherhood

INSIDE VIEW OF
Faith Tabernacle
OUTSIDE VIEW OF FAITH TABERNACLE
CHURCH MASS TRANSIT— Over 250 buses commuting the worshippers to Church from all nook and crannies of Lagos & environs
Dr. David Oyedepo is the founding president of the Living Faith Church Worldwide Inc. And senior pastor of the Faith Tabernacle, a 50,000 capacity sanctuary located in Canaan Land, Ota, a suburb of Lagos Nigeria.
The construction of this gigantic architectural masterpiece was completed within twelve months and dedicated on September 18, 1999. Built totally debt free and without any foreign inputs! To God alone be all the glory.
Today, Faith Tabernacle stands as the home of signs and wonders for men and women all over the world who keep coming in droves to worship the King of kings and Lord of lords, Jesus Christ the Son of the Living God.
Visit our website for more information: www.davidoyedepoministries.org

Aerial View Of Covenant University

College of Business & Social Sciences

More Facilities@ Covenant University

College of Science & Technology

University Library (Centre For Learning Resources)

4,000 Seat Students Chapel

More Facilities@ Covenant University

Post Graduate Building

Senior Staff Residential Quarters

Covenant University 100 Room Ultra Modern Guest House

Students Hall Of Residence

More Facilities@Landmark University

University Chapel

College Building

Cafetaria

More Facilities@Landmark University

One of the Student's Halls Of Residence

Professors Village

Staff Quarters